Handbook for Teaching Hmong-Speaking Students

developed by

Bruce Thowpaou Bliatout, Ph.D.
Bruce T. Downing, Ph.D.
Judy Lewis
Dao Yang, Ph.D.

Publishing Information

This handbook was funded in part with funds from the Transition Program for Refugee Children, education funds authorized under the Refugee Act of 1980. The opinions expressed herein do not, however, necessarily reflect the position or policy of the U.S. government, and no official endorsement should be inferred. The document was developed at the request of the California State Department of Education Bilingual Education Office, as part of a series of handbooks for teaching language minority students. The handbook was prepared for publication with desktop publishing equipment provided under an educational grant from Apple Computer, Inc. to Folsom Cordova Unified School District. The manuscript was prepared on a Macintosh Plus, using Microsoft Word and Aldus Pagemaker, and run on a Laserwriter Plus. The cover screen is from a photograph of a *paj ntaub* designed and sewn in Ban Vinai refugee camp, Thailand, circa 1983; from the collection of Lue Vang. The handbook was printed by Spilman Printing Company, 1801-9th Street, Sacramento, CA 95814.

Copies of this handbook are available for $4.50 each, plus sales tax for California residents, and $.75 per copy shipping ($5.52 total for California residents, $4.77 for out of state residents) from Folsom Cordova Unified School District, Southeast Asia Community Resource Center, 125 East Bidwell Street, Folsom, CA 95630, telephone (916) 635-6815 or 985-4483.

Contents

List of Figures

List of Tables

Foreword

Folsom Cordova Unified School District, which serves three distinct communities at the outskirts of suburban Sacramento, has faced rapid unexpected changes in the ethnic, linguistic, and socioeconomic makeup of its student population over the past ten to fifteen years. Those of us serving this district's students, for the most part, were trained before college teacher credential programs offered courses in second language acquisition, cultural diversity, and adaptation to life in a new country. The arrival of a few Vietnamese refugee students between 1975 and 1979 introduced the district's personnel to the challenges and rewards of teaching language minority students. The community resettled about 10% of Sacramento County's newly arriving refugees during the period 1979 to 1981, resulting in twenty to forty new students, kindergarten through twelfth grade, enrolling each month. These students, also from Vietnam, were of a different language group, ethnically, culturally, and socioeconomically unlike the earlier students.

Elementary students were enrolled at ten different schools, keeping a family's children all at one school whenever possible, and coordinating a school's language needs with bilingual aides from a central pool that served schools on an itinerant basis. We found that elementary students were interacting, learning English, and within a fairly short period of time, comparable to classmates academically; what also happened was that the resident staff, students, and community members had for the first time an opportunity to know and work with children from backgrounds quite different from the ones they knew. Individual teachers, aides, volunteers, and specialists took an interest in the newcomer students and some began to develop areas of expertise, and to communicate with others about the problems and successes of these new students.

Later, in 1982, yet another group came to our community: the Hmong from rural Laos. Instead of reacting with dismay, schools embraced the newest of the new, and with the assistance of talented Hmong community members, began to learn how these students were similar to, and different from, those who had come before.

Our district, like many others in the state, has come face to face with California's new student population, with little preparation and few resources. The Asian and Minority Language Group Project of the California State Department of Education's Bilingual Education Office provides a valuable educational resource to classroom teachers, specialists, and administrators serving the language minority students within an ongoing program. We are pleased to work cooperatively with Van LE and other consultants at the Bilingual Education Office, as it is at the district and school level that the "ideal" educational programs are refined and reshaped by practical experience.

We, as individuals in the school community, have been enriched by the diverse talents, skills, attitudes, behaviors, and world views of peoples from so many backgrounds, and we are proud to recognize their importance in tomorrow's California with the Southeast Asia Community Resource Center, and the collaboration on the production of this handbook.

David H. Benson
Superintendent
Folsom Cordova Unified School District
January 1988

Preface

This handbook was developed as part of the Asian and Minority Language Group Project in the Bilingual Education Office, California State Department of Education. The project was designed to assist school districts in providing effective bilingual education services to language minority students. The Project Team identified as its first major activity the development of handbooks for a number or Asian and minority language groups.

The purpose of these handbooks is to assist school personnel in understanding selected Asian and minority language groups. The handbooks have been designed for use by bilingual education specialists as well as administrators and teachers who have more general responsibilities for the education of language minority students.

Chapter I and II of this handbook address general background factors regarding the Hmong-speaking language group: immigration history, educational background, and sociocultural factors. Chapters III and IV contain specific information regarding the Hmong language and appropriate program offerings that will promote the academic achievement of Hmong-speaking students.

This handbook is complemented by other publications developed by the Bilingual Education Office, including *Schooling and Language Minority Students: A Theoretical Framework*,[i] which provides extensive information regarding bilingual education theory and practice. It also outlines the basic principles underlying successful bilingual education programs and suggests a variety of implementation strategies.

The analyses and illustrations in the *Theoretical Framework* are not specific to particular language groups. Rather, the *Theoretical Framework* provides a way of conceptualizing and organizing appropriate program services based on program goals, available resources, community background factors, and student characteristics.

This handbook and others developed as part of the Asian and Minority Language Group Project are designed to assist school district personnel in better understanding specific Asian and minority language group communities and individual students who come from these communities.[ii] We believe that by using this handbook in conjunction

---

[i] Information regading this publication is available from the Evaluation, Dissemination, and Assessment Center, California State University, Los Angeles, 5151 State University Drive, Los Angeles, CA 90032. The Center also has handbooks on Vietnamese-speaking and Korean-speaking students.

[ii] Handbooks on Cantonese-speaking, Japanese-speaking, Pilipino-speaking, and Portuguese-speaking students are available from the Bureau of

with the *Theoretical Framework*, school personnel should be able to develop program services that are appropriately suited to the needs of individual Hmong-speaking students.

The Asian and Minority Language Group Project Team of the Bilingual Education Office began development of this handbook in June, 1985. It went through several drafts and was revised by teachers, linguists, and members of the language group community before publication. Every effort has been made to create a handbook that would be useful to educators who are responsible for the education of Hmong-speaking students.

In spite of extensive work done by many individuals on this handbook, it should be regarded as a first edition. As time and resources permit, efforts will be made to refine it. It is difficult in one volume to depict the uniqueness and heterogeneity that characterizes the Hmong language group. The reader should recognize that any language group is complex and diverse, with individual members and generations having a variety of needs and characteristics based on different experiences in America and in their native countries.

This handbook represents an initial attempt to describe generally the needs and characteristics of the Hmong language group. Much more research and developmental work needs to be done by all who are responsible for ensuring the successful adaptation to America by minority language groups.

Leo R. Lopez
Manager
Bilingual Education Office
California State Department of Education
Sacramento, January 1988

Publications Sales, California State Department of Education, P.O. Box 271, Sacramento, CA 95801-0271 (phone: 916-445-1260).

Acknowledgements

The Bilingual Education Office of the California State Department of Education wishes to recognize the many individuals who assisted in completing this handbook. The facilitator, Judy Lewis, coordinator of the Transitional English Program Office, Folsom Cordova Unified School District, worked closely with the project team in keeping the handbook on schedule and making revisions to the drafts. As a result of her knowledge of the Hmong language and culture, Ms. Lewis was able to follow closely the development of the handbook and write suggestions concerning the implications of the contents to teachers.

Bruce Thowpaou Bliatout, Health Program Coordinator, Multnomah County Health Division, Portland, Oregon, Bruce T. Downing, Associate Professor of Linguistics and ESL, University of Minnesota, and Dao Yang, Counselor Advocate at the General College, University of Minnesota, were the principal writers of this handbook. They spent an inestimable amount of time in meeting, collecting data, doing extensive research, and writing sections of the handbook. Space does not permit listing the many interested members of the language group community who suggested improvements for various drafts.

This handbook was developed as part of the Asian and Minority Language Group Project of the Bilingual Education Office. Office staff reviewed drafts and made suggestions to the writers. David Dolson, Assistant Manager, and Daniel Holt, Consultant, made editorial comments on the manuscripts. Van LE, as Team Leader, provided overall coordination of the development of this handbook.

The Bilingual Education Office also acknowledges Robert Weidenhamer, Director of Elementary Education, Folsom Cordova Unified School District, for working closely with this Office in providing technical assistance to language minority students and to the Board of Education for accepting a special sub-grant from the Transition Program for Refugee Children which supported the production of this handbook.

Van LE
Hmong Handbook Project Team Leader
Bilingual Education Office
California StateDepartment of Education
January 1988

x

Note to Readers

In the preparation of this handbook the authors have attempted to provide information that would be helpful to teachers and administrators working with Hmong students and their parents. Chapter 4 deals directly with instructional strategies for Hmong and English language development. To bring out the relevance and applicability of information elsewhere in the text, boxes with the heading *"Implications for Educators"* have been inserted into the text wherever appropriate. Since these implications and teaching hints are based on the main text, that should be read first. But the boxes will be the place to look later when you are searching for practical suggestions.

❖ ❖ ❖ ❖ ❖ ❖ ❖ ❖ ❖ ❖ ❖ ❖ ❖ ❖ ❖ ❖

Background of the Hmong People

The Hmong in Laos and as Refugees

❖Origins of the Hmong

Since 1975, the United States has been enriched by a new and unique group of people. They speak their own language and possess their own traditions and culture, and they have a desire to contribute their share to the multicultural society that is the United States of America. They came to this country from the plateaus of northern Laos. They say that they lived above the clouds and they were the first to see the sun rise and the last to watch the sun set. These people, referred to as Miao or Meo by others, call themselves the Hmong.

The Hmong constitute one of the most ancient peoples in Asia. Since the Hmong language had never been written until the 20th century, we have few documents of Hmong history before that period. According to their tales and popular songs, the ancestors of the Hmong had been living in the central part of present-day China since prehistoric times. Like many other peoples they established villages and built fortified towns along the rivers, in the fertile valleys and rich plains. For their livelihood, they grew crops and raised domestic animals. They drew strength to defend themselves against their enemies from a structured system of clans and a strong consciousness of their ethnic identity. From some period of prosperity in the remote past have come many rich Hmong traditions, such as folk tales and songs, marriage and funeral rites, instrumental music and musical instruments.

But at some point, these peaceful Hmong peasants began to be attacked by invaders from the North, the Han Chinese. A bloody and deadly time of strife ensued, pitting the Hmong against the invaders. Finally, around the middle of the 18th century, the Hmong were defeated by the troops of the Chinese Empire. Many of these survivors

1

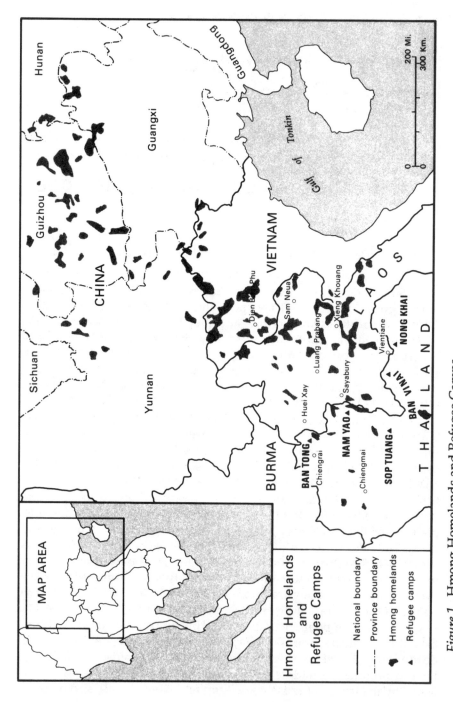

Figure 1 Hmong Homelands and Refugee Camps.
Copyright © Center for Migration Studies of New York. Used with permission.
(By Carol Gersmehl, in *The Hmong in Transition.* New York: Center for Migration Studies of New York, 1986: xv.)

2

eventually faced humiliation, imprisonment, and death. Thousands of families undertook an historic migration southward through the mountains, constantly fighting to defend themselves.

Most of the fugitive Hmong came to settle in the highlands of south China. Others crossed the border into northern Vietnam, establishing themselves in the hills there. Still others pushed their migration further toward the west, into the landlocked country of Laos, always searching for a place where they might remain free and at peace. Those who reached Laos from southern China are the ancestors of the Hmong who have recently come to America in the same quest for freedom (Larteguy and Yang, 1978).

❖The Hmong in Laos

The first Hmong groups entered northeastern Laos around 1810-1820. That part of the country was covered with mountains forests, with a sparse human population, but rich with game. The newcomers settled near the highest summits, not wishing to trouble any local population or administration. They built their houses with wood and bamboo and covered them with elephant grass or with palm leaves. Because of the geographic conditions, they had to give up their ancestors' agricultural system of lowland farming and adopt the "slash and burn" method of farming. This method involved clearing an area of the forest and then setting it on fire. The soil, fertilized by the ashes, was used to produce successive crops of rice, corn, and a wide variety of vegetables and other crops. The Hmong raised chickens, pigs, oxen, and horses. They also grew hemp with which they made clothing for the whole family and grew opium poppies as a cash crop for trade and for their own medicinal needs. Periodically families and whole villages would move, to burn off a fresh parcel of land. Thus, for decades, they organized their life in almost complete self-sufficiency.

Soon after their arrival in Laos, the Hmong migrants made themselves accepted by the local authorities by offering gifts and by demonstrating their peaceful attitudes. Little by little, they gained sympathy and friendship among the Lao and other ethnic groups of Laos. As the families grew up and the groups developed, the Hmong community constantly needed to extend their agricultural areas. By 1972, the Hmong population had reached 300,000 people, ten percent of the total population of the country. They were scattered through ten provinces of northern and central Laos: Phongsali, Houakhong, Luang Prabang, Houaphanh, Xiengkhouang, Sayaboury, Vangvieng, Vien-

3

tiane, Borikhane, and Khammouane. In 1947, the new Lao constitution recognized the Hmong as full members of the community of Laos, which became independent of France in 1954.

Implications for Educators:

Hmong living in different areas have different traditions and customs. Questions like *Why do Hmong ...?* or *Are Hmong....?* are difficult for a Hmong to answer. Most people know how things were done in their own region, but cannot speak for all Hmong. Keep in mind there was no mass communication or libraries of resource materials from which people gained knowledge and generalizations. Often Hmong parents and students will first learn from resource materials which educators make available to them; unfortunately, few of them are written by Hmong about themselves, rather by outsiders who have a different perspective.

As Laotian citizens, the Hmong contributed to the defense of the country, under the Royal Lao Government. After World War II they were involved as partisans against the Pathet Lao and the Viet Minh coalition. During the "Secret War of Laos" (1961-1973) they fought as "Special Forces" with American military backing against the North Vietnamese divisions that were invading the Plain of Jars and the northeastern provinces of the country, which adjoin North Vietnam. The United States government trained, equipped, and financed these Special Forces, which were directed by Laotian Royal Army Forces with U.S. support.

Thousands of Hmong were killed in defending their homeland. Almost all the Hmong villages were burned, their cattle destroyed and their agricultural fields devastated. During this time one third of the Hmong population of Laos became "displaced persons". Most of them survived on rations provided by the military to the husbands or sons who served in the army. Others received some food assistance from the Laotian Government, which was supported by the United States in its struggle against the Communist Pathet Lao and North Vietnamese.

On February 21, 1973, the Royal Lao Government and the Pathet Lao signed a political agreement in Vientiane, temporarily ending the suffering of the Hmong and many other people across the country. A "Government of National Union" was formed on April 4, 1974, receiving enthusiastic support throughout the multicultural Laotian nation. The Hmong, too, strongly supported its policy of national reconciliation.

❖Fleeing Laos as Political Refugees

The peace that came to Laos during this period did not last long. In May, 1975, immediately after the communist military victory in Cambodia and South Vietnam, the Pathet Lao violated the "Treaty of Peace and National Reconciliation" and took power in Laos. They arrested the non-communist leaders who still remained in the country and sent thousands of politicians, military and administrative officers, technicians and ordinary citizens to political re-education camps. On December 2, the Pathet Lao abolished the Lao monarchy and proclaimed the Lao People's Democratic Republic. Then they started a bloody repression against the Hmong, accusing them of being C.I.A. mercenaries during the Secret War of Laos.

As a consequence the Hmong began to leave their villages, individually or in family groups, to escape across the border into Thailand. The Pathet Lao tried to stop the Hmong people's flight by killing them in ambush, mining their paths, and sending captives back to their remote villages. Despite danger, disease, starvation and death, a number of them succeeded in crossing the Mekong River, often under the Pathet Lao fire, in search of safety. (For more on the aftermath of the war in Laos and the flight of the Hmong, see Yang, 1980, 1982, 1984a, 1984b).

There are 13,103 Hmong children now enrolled in California schools (Spring 1987 Language Census). Their families are survivors of this experience.

❖Refugee Camps in Thailand

The Hmong along with another ethnic group, the Thai Dam, were the first refugee groups to arrive in Thailand, beginning in May, 1975.

They were rapidly followed by the Khmu, the Mien and other hill-tribes. Finally lowland Lao also followed the same path, fleeing the Pathet Lao regime. Several camps were eventually created in Thai territory to accommodate these fugitives from Laos.

Namphong was the first Hmong refugee center. It was a former military camp, surrounded by barbed wire, and was located in the northeast of Thailand in an isolated area in the middle of the forest. Opened on May 10, 1975, it sheltered about 12,500 refugees by the end of that year. Early in 1976, the center was relocated to Ban Vinai, in a hilly region close to the Lao border.[1] This camp was built by the refugees themselves, with U.S. Government funds, under the supervision of the Royal Thai Government. It was about 200 acres in size and was divided into five centers, each with its own center staff. Despite an increasing number of departures to third countries, Ban Vinai continued to expand with new arrivals and the transfer of refugee populations from other camps. In 1986, Ban Vinai extended over nine centers, spread out over 400 acres, and sheltered about 45,000 Hmong refugees (Minnesota Governor's Advisory Council for Refugees, 1986). These people were still hoping desperately for permission to be resettled in the United States, in France, in Australia, or in Canada, or dreaming of returning to Laos, under new political conditions.

Facing an ever greater influx of people coming from all parts of Laos, the Thai Government was forced to open new refugee camps, scattered along the Thai and Lao border. In March, 1976, Nongkhai, located at the Thai border, opposite Vientiane, the capital of Laos, counted about 8,000 Lao and 10,500 Hmong, living in two separate communities. Pua, another camp in Nan Province, held 11,000 refugees at

---

Implications for Educators:

The group of 8,000 Hmong due to arrive in the United States during 1987 may have been at Ban Vinai for up to ten years. The young children born in Thailand have grown up in an environment of crowding, poor sanitation, idleness, authoritarianism, and dependency. They and their parents will probably have different needs than the groups of Hmong who spent less time in the camp environment. The older children (entering junior high or senior high here) had the opportunity to pay for English lessons, using the English 900 series, levels 1-5. Until recently, they learned Thai and Hmong in the camp run classes; the Thai government has recently discouraged the teaching of Thai and English, to reduce false hopes of resettling in Thailand or the United States.

---

[1]Dao Yang's personal notes, taken while in Thai refugee camps in 1975-76.

the same period of time, mostly Hmong from Sayaboury and Luang Prabang provinces. Other centers such as Ubone, in the south, particularly designated for lowland Lao, and Outradith and Chiangkhong, in the north, for Hmong, Mien, Khmu and other ethnic groups, also welcomed an increasing number of refugees from Laos. During the peak period, in 1980, more than 1,200 Hmong and 2,400 ethnic Lao arrived monthly in Thailand. Since Nongkhai and Ubone camps were closed in 1982, two new camps have been opened: Chiangkham (7,000 Hmong and 6,000 Lao, Thai Dam and Khmu) and Napho (43,000 ethnic Lao). It is generally estimated that since May 1975, more than 300,000 people, of whom 130,000 are Hmong, have left Laos to seek asylum abroad.

Hmong Resettlement in the U. S.

In January, 1976, some 150 Hmong families, numbering about 750 people, formed the first Hmong contingent coming from the Thai refugee camps to the United States, under the *Indochina Migration and Refugee Assistance Act of 1975* (PL 9423). The heads of those families had been employed by the United States Agency for International Development (USAID) or by the U.S. Embassy in Vientiane during the Secret War of Laos. Their previous service to the U.S. government had obtained for them the special privilege of immigrating to America. Those Hmong families and others that followed were helped in their resettlement by churches, non-profit organizations or individuals who acted as American sponsors. This is how the Hmong resettlement in the United States began.

But most Hmong were admitted to the United States because of their association with the United States during the Secret War. Organized in special guerilla units, they had acted as a line of defense between the Communist-controlled Plain of Jars in northern Laos and Vientiane, the capital; they directed air strikes for U.S. bombers stationed in Thailand, and they rescued downed American pilots. It was because of these wartime activities that the Hmong became targets for retaliation after the Communist take-over in 1975. The United States government, having involved the Hmong people in its Indochina war, felt a responsibility for their subsequent fate and welcomed a great number of them to this country. After the Hmong refugees who had close military involvement with the United States had been granted asylum in this country, they were able to submit petitions on behalf of close relatives who had been left behind. So their relatives were also able to leave the camps in Thailand. Following a peak period in the years 1979-80, the influx of Hmong refugees to California and other states has continued at a slow pace into the late 1980's.

❖Hmong Population Centers in the U.S.

When the first Hmong groups came to the United States, they lived in small communities of 200 to 500 people scattered across the

Table 1
Population of Hmong in Selected States, January, 1987

California	47,000
Wisconsin	13,200
Minnesota	10,500
Michigan	2,500
Rhode Island	2,300
Colorado	2,000
Oregon	1,100
Illinois	1,000
Georgia	700
Pennsylvania	500
Kansas	500
Texas	450
Washington	450
North Carolina	400
Ohio	400
Oklahoma	400
South Carolina	350
Nebraska	250
Tennessee	250
Alabama	200
Indiana	200
Utah	150
Nevada	100
Virginia	50
South Dakota	30

Estimates given to Dao Yang by Hmong refugee leaders in each state, 1987, and in California the sum of county estimates given by community leaders.

United States. There were Hmong in Philadelphia, Pennsylvania; Missoula, Montana; Santa Ana and Long Beach, California; Des Moines, Iowa; St. Paul, Minnesota; Denver, Colorado; Spartanburg, South Carolina; Honolulu, Hawaii; and other towns and cities. Following the massive influx of Hmong in 1979-80, the geographic distribution of the Hmong population in this country has been constantly changing. Some Hmong communities appeared in other states. Almost immediately Hmong who had initially been placed in a certain community by the resettlement process began to relocate elsewhere. This Hmong secondary migration brought the Hmong population in California to over 47,000 people at the end of 1986 and gave the state the largest Hmong population in the United States. Minnesota, which held the largest single Hmong community in 1981, saw its Hmong population reduced from 12,000 to 9,000 by 1984, then increased again to 10,000 in 1985 (Minnesota Governor's Advisory Council for Refugees, 1986). On the other hand, Wisconsin, which numbered 6,500 Hmong in 1984, saw this immigrant population increase gradually to 13,231 people by January, 1987. Populations by states as of January, 1987, are shown in Table 1.

In all more than 60,000 Hmong from Laos have been resettled in the United States between 1975 and 1986. An additional 8,000 were expected to arrive from Thailand camps in 1987. To this number must be added 25,000 or more Hmong children born in this country.

Implications for Educators:

The children born in the United States are not refugees, and therefore do not qualify for special programs funded under U.S. refugee programs. Children born here may have received less contact with public health nurses, and may not have received all their childhood immunizations. Entry into school is the first time children are checked for immunizations, and shots are often begun at this time. The need for childhood immunizations is relevant to parent education programs.

Children born here have social security numbers and birth certificates; those born overseas have either an immigration document, an alien registration card, or citizenship papers. The birth date assigned by the officials in the camps is legal, but often inaccurate. School decisions are often based on chronological age; for example, many special education tests are based on age norms. To verify a birth date, a bilingual person should interview the parents to help establish the actual time of birth; sometimes the closest accurate date may be something like *after the corn harvest in in the year before we escaped to Thailand.*

❖Hmong Migration to California

The Hmong population of California, now the largest in the United States, began with the resettlement in January, 1976, of a few Hmong families who had been closely associated with the U.S. involvement in the Laotian Secret War. Progressively, other Hmong families came from the refugee camps in Thailand. One Hmong man, a former pilot, describes a rather typical experience.

> *My family and I arrived in Santa Ana on September 9, 1976. There were 500-600 Hmong in Orange County, 250-300 in Los Angeles, 80-100 in Santa Barbara, 20-30 in San Jose, 100-120 in San Francisco, 20-30 in Sacramento, and 100-200 in San Diego. Four days after my arrival in California, I got a job in a company. I worked there for three months before I was offered a position as a social worker by the Orange County Welfare Office. But my cousin and my brother-in-law were unable to find a job in the Orange County area because of their lack of English. So on May 25, 1977, my family and I moved to Planada, Merced County, in hopes of having the opportunity for all of us to find farm work. Soon after, we began to work on a farm and in the fruit orchards. Our wish was to lead a quiet life, far away from the tensions of the big city.*

By the end of May, 1977, this man's younger brother left his home in Virginia, with his family, and went to join the small Hmong community in Planada. Two days later, another family of relatives arrived from Pennsylvania. By the middle of June, thirteen Hmong families, about eighty people, had been resettled in Merced County. It was summertime and s there was no school. All the children above twelve years old participated in the harvesting of produce and the picking of fruit, contributing as they were able to improve the financial situation of their families. Being able to support themselves, these two brothers and the cousin who had joined them submitted a petition in favor of their relatives still in the Thai refugee camps to the State Department. In 1978-79, some of these started to arrive in the Central Valley, preceding the vast Hmong secondary migration to California which began in 1980.

❖Reasons for Secondary Migration

Several factors explained this Hmong secondary migration. First of all, the successful economic experience of a Hmong farmer in Fresno in 1979 coincided with the general unemployment situation of the Hmong throughout the United States during a time of economic recession and of major cuts in funding for refugee services by the U.S. Government.

Early in 1980, Hmong men from all parts of the country who had heard reports of this farmer's success went to Fresno to visit the fortunate Hmong farmer and ask his advice. There they found the weather milder, more pleasant and more attractive because of the similarity to what they had known in the mountains of Laos. Many of these migrants went back home and held council with their families and other members of their clans about moving to the Fresno area. Rapidly the news spread, crossed the local communities and reached other areas. Many people decided to move to California. Most of them hoped to find a plot of land and to become economically self-sufficient as soon as possible. Some left their jobs, and even may have sold a house, to take part in the migration, under family pressure. Some, not wanting to live isolated from relatives and friends, followed the majority. From all parts of the country, by successive waves, the Hmong began to converge on the Central Valley. The Hmong population in Fresno, which was about thirty people in July, 1979, increased to 2,000 in December, 1980. One year later, the number was about 7,000. In December, 1982, it had reached 12,000. After that date, the migration began to decrease, reaching a stable level in 1985.

Implications for Educators:

School personnel often overlook the influence of success stories and tales of misfortune that circulate on the well-developed national Hmong grapevine. In a society which has existed for centuries without written communication, this oral method of learning news and profiting from the experience or misfortune of others is highly developed. When school personnel hope that parents will agree to certain programs for their children, it is helpful to be aware of the oral network, and to locate other examples of success within the Hmong, or non-Hmong, community, from which parents can learn.

The distribution of Hmong in California cities with the largest Hmong populations, as reported by Hmong leaders in 1987, is as shown in Table 2.

Table 2 Distribution of Hmong in California Cities, 1987

Fresno	18,500
Merced	6,500
Stockton	6,500
Sacramento	4,000
San Diego	3,500
Banning	1,200
Santa Ana	1,200
Yuba City	1,200
Visalia	750
Modesto	650
Long Beach	600
Eureka	480
Porterville	400
Tulare	400
Fairfield	300
Riverside	300
Santa Barbara	300
Oroville	200

Estimates given to Dao Yang by Hmong refugee leaders in California, 1987.

Table 3
**ENROLLMENT OF HMONG STUDENTS IN
CALIFORNIA SCHOOLS, 1981 TO 1987**

CENSUS	LEP	FEP	TOTAL
Spring 1981	1,185	142	1,327
Spring 1982	3,036	335	3,371
Spring 1983	4,705	748	5,453
Spring 1984	6,457	1,244	7,701
Spring 1985	7,798	1,428	9,226
Spring 1986	8,784	1,932	10,716
Spring 1987	10,780	2,323	13,103

DATA BICAL Report No. 87-7N. Sacramento: California State Department of Education, Bilingual Education Office, Spring 1987.

There are also smaller Hmong populations in other California cities including San Jose, Chico, Crescent City, Redding, Santa Rosa, Bakersfield, Madera, Richmond, and San Francisco. Populations are increasing rapidly in some of these locations. Reported state-wide enrollments of Hmong children in California schools from 1981 to 1987 are shown in Table 3.

In recent years some Hmong living in Fresno, Merced, and Stockton have moved again to other small towns, particularly to the north in California, in the hope of finding better employment opportunities. Many of them are concerned to give their children the opportunity to mingle with more native English-speaking children in the schools.

Implications for Educators:

Most Hmong families have moved many times, and programs designed for migrant education, with clear entry placement criteria and short term objectives that transfer to many basal programs may help overcome the negative effects of frequent moves. Building resource networks for paraprofessionals, consultants, and materials development, in which districts share personnel and materials across district boundaries, may decrease the amount of start up time required in districts with new Hmong populations. Educating parents about the ways in which school districts differ from each other, and how family decisions affect the success of children in school is important.

Factors that affect transiency are often not known to the school personnel, including the sale of rental units, the availability of low-income housing for large families, community tensions, and differing public assistance programs.

Worldwide Hmong Population

Besides those still living in their original homeland in China, there are now Hmong people who have settled in northern Vietnam, in Thailand, and even in Burma, as well as Laos. The flight of refugees from Laos has scattered Hmong people to a number of different countries outside of Asia. It is now estimated that there are 5,864,150 Hmong in the world, distributed as follows:

Table 4 Approximate Hmong Population in the World

China	5,031,000
Laos	200,000
Vietnam	400,000
Thailand	140,000*
United States	85,000
France	7,000**
Canada	650
Australia	350
Argentina	150

*Including 60,000 Hmong refugees from Laos
**Including French Guiana
1982 census in the People's Republic of China, and best available estimates.

Chapter 2

Education in Laos, in Thai Refugee Camps, and in the United States

Factors in Laos

❖Traditional Village Education

Since their diaspora started two hundred years ago in China, the Hmong people have constantly tried their best, wherever they find themselves, to preserve their cultural heritage, the guarantor of their own identity. Even though they did not have any writing system, they handed down their knowledge and traditions from one generation to another.

When Hmong children grow up back in Laos, they start to learn about what surrounds them by sight, touch and hearing under the close watch of the parents and grandparents. Thus they quickly become familiarized with the family house and its domestic animals. Early in their life, children accompany their parents to the fields, and begin to learn how to grow crops by observing adults at work. After dinner, they spend hours, close to the family fireplace, listening to the elderly relate Hmong history or recount Hmong legends and folk tales. These long evenings, which end only when sleep comes, help the Hmong children to develop their vocabulary, to diversify their knowledge, to improve their communication skills, and to sharpen their intelligence. The children benefit from extensive exposure to the language and the experience of adults.

The father has the task of teaching the sons how to become mature men. This is done principally through letting the sons watch, and then try things for themselves under the watchful and critical eye of the father. The father's attitude is more one of critical guidance than of praise for the sake of encouragement. Thus the father shows his sons how to repair an agricultural tool, how to raise horses and

---

Implications for Educators:

With television and homework, there is less time for children to listen to adults tell stories, legends, and history. What this means is less exposure to complex and abstract Hmong language. The children can function socially in the home language, but are limited in expressing complex ideas. When English language development is also limited, the children have no vehicle for expressing their thoughts. Often, encouragement by the teacher can increase both the amount of language use by the parents, and the degree of participation by the children. Rather than tell the students, *Speak English at home*, encourage parents to develop their children's native language skills.

---

cattle, how to choose land for farming, how to hunt deer or tigers with a flint-lock, and how to deal with family business. He often brings them to community meetings where they are able to learn about social problems, economic issues and political events, and where they can observe the ways adults solve community and family problems.

Implications for Educators:

General praise to encourage students (*Good job reading*) is not as necessary as specific instruction and re-teaching. Parents consider the correcting of errors an important part of teaching; students will know they've done a "good job" when they succeed. The teacher should be sure the student knows the criteria of success; knows specifically what is wrong; and knows how to correct what is wrong. As an example:

❖ *Teacher:* Read this paragraph out loud. Start here and end here. I'm going to listen for the ending sounds on words.

❖ *Student:* (Reads paragraph, enunciating carefully. Drops the end sounds on five words.)

❖ *Teacher:* You missed this one, this one, ...(lightly marks missed words). Now read silently while I read out loud. (Teacher reads out loud). Now you try it again.

❖ *Student:* (Reads it again)

❖ *Teacher:* Great, you got all five. Now listen while Charlie reads the next paragraph, and see if he gets all the end sounds.

As for the mother, she also has a specific role to play toward her daughters. She teaches them how to keep the house clean, how to prepare family meals, how to take care of the chickens and pigs, and how to become a good wife. Often after dinner, the daughters help their mother pound rice, and usually they go to bed late in the evening. They generally are up again before dawn to assist her in drawing water from the spring, in milling corn at the village millstone, and in cooking for the whole family. Thus, children of both sexes, despite a lack of formal education, receive in their remote villages an education of this sort, which traditionally prepares each new generation for their future responsibilities.

❖Typical Hmong Adult's Educational Experience

Although in traditional Hmong society most individuals did not attend school or formal classes, the Hmong culture had alternative standards for what was considered "educated". This education consisted of learning various levels of ceremonial and religious rituals. Each son would have to become proficient to a certain minimum level in traditional oral rituals before being considered a head of household. Most boys learned from their fathers, uncles, or grandfathers. This is because Hmong families, while each following the broad outlines of ancestor worship and animistic beliefs, have their own specific individual rituals. These rituals must be performed exactly to the last detail or bad luck and/or illness may occur in family members. Even within the same clan, different branches may follow slightly different family rituals. The closer in ritual families are to each other, the closer they consider the relationship (Chindarsi, 1976). Families within one clan, who follow the same rituals to the last detail, consider themselves to be part of one large family and can count on each other for social and economic support of all kinds. The heads of these households are called brothers. An average Hmong head of household is educated in performing the following simple ceremonies: naming of infants, calling of souls, performing New Year's rituals, worshipping ancestors, and worshipping nature spirits.

Those who wish to broaden their education can select various fields of study. Some may choose to master traditional singing, which consists of learning to create more and more complex rhyming. Others may choose to learn more advanced religious ceremonies and rituals. Still others may choose to study the Hmong qeej instrument, learning the stories and legends of the Hmong race, the verses for religious ceremonies and rituals, and how to entertain others for pleasure. Lastly, some may choose to study the Hmong traditional healing arts, of which there are several branches—herbology, acupuncture, massage, scraping and cupping, and diagnosis. While there is no formal structure of any of these studies nor any certificate or degree bestowed on any of the students, the Hmong society nevertheless bestows a higher status on persons proficient in any of the above-mentioned fields.

❖Oral Language Development

The Hmong have always placed an emphasis on oral skills as there were no writing skills to fall back on. People in the Hmong society achieved high social status not only because of wealth or education, but because of the ability to speak well during social occasions, religious ceremonies, and other political and legal events. In traditional Hmong society it was necessary to learn from elders how to speak in the correct manner for these types of occasions. This more formal mode of conversation, while of course being in the Hmong language, nevertheless was different and considered a "higher level of speaking" than everyday language. It made use of some special vocabulary that was not understood by everyone. Regional, village, clan, and family leaders could only become such if skilled in this method of communication; thus, families encouraged their youth, particularly boys, to become proficient in oral skills.

Learning how to create verses as a way to communicate with others was considered an important part of the Hmong culture. As an example, during the Hmong New Year season which is also a courtship period, girls and boys line up in a field and toss balls to each other, all the while exchanging verses as a way to get to know each other and begin romantic alliances. From as early as the first year of life, Hmong children begin to learn how to create verses from their parents, grandparents, and older siblings. Girls in particular try hard to become proficient in this skill as the society considers this a very desirable attribute. Boys also learn to create verses that are sung during marriage, naming, religious, and funeral services which in the Hmong society are the responsibilities of the males. Girls' skills are to sing and to speak well in order to attract a husband and create a harmonious household, whereas for the boys it is to represent the family and the clan to the outside community, to assume leadership and to be able to defend their clan in court.

The Lao school system reinforced the Hmong traditional belief that in order to succeed in life one had to be able to speak well, in front of the teacher and class, in front of the family and clan, in front of village members, and most important of all, in front of visiting dignitaries and/or government officials. The schooling system in Laos placed a great emphasis on memorization and the recitation of set texts.

Implications for Educators.

Familiar techniques can be readily transferred to assignments in American classes. There is a great deal of pattern to the speaking done within the society; a person learns the appropriate structure, vocabulary, and "flower words", then varies the text to give it a personal signature. Students will fare better in preparing speeches, reports, letters, or essays if they are given a sample, which can be memorized and then varied to suit the specific circumstances and personal style. This technique runs counter to American teachers' desire not to stifle creativity, but provides a structure and familiar technique for learning public language, whether oral or written.

This same strategy can be applied to other kinds of learning. Any memorization should pair auditory with tactile or visual channels. Math facts can be learned by recitation; mnemonic devices are helpful; any kind of patterned, rhyming, rhythmic speech will parallel traditional ways of learning information. (It should be noted that rhyming in Hmong is different than rhyming in English; words rhyme when they contain the same vowel and the same tone, rather than the same vowels and end sounds. *Paj* and *vaj* rhyme.)

When learning by auditory means is impractical, visual patterning as in charts or grids may be helpful for learning. Drawing on shapes, symbols, and colors from traditional Hmong costume may aid the discrimination and memory when paired with visual material.

In general, learning is accomplished by "seeing and doing". Whenever possible, teachers should employ this traditional learning strategy. Demonstrate what is to be done, let the student try, correct the errors, then let the student try again.

❖Traditional Child Rearing Practices

Traditional Hmong society placed a great emphasis on having many children. Parents devoted most of their time and energy to providing for and fostering their children. Since Hmong society places family values above individual concerns, most Hmong parents spent the majority of every day in close physical proximity with their children. The children would accompany their parents to and from the rice fields, to fetch water from the river, and around the village. In general, Hmong parents carry and fondle their children more than is common in Western cultures. Thus, it is a frequent sight to see either a Hmong mother or father with a baby tied to his or her back in a gaily embroidered baby carrier. Up until about the ages of three or four, most

Hmong children would never be out of sight of at least one of their parents and would spend much of their time playing while their parents worked. As early as five or six years of age, some children would be assisting their parents with simple tasks around the house and in the fields.

Most Lao schools allowed children to enter first grade at age seven. Since many Hmong families did not keep formal records of when infants were born, many did not know at what time a child became seven years old. It was common folk practice among the Hmong that a child was ready to attend school if he or she could touch his or her left ear with his or her right hand, with the right arm lifted up over the head. As children turned six or seven, parents would have to decide whether the child would be selected to go to school. In general, if unable to send all their children, parents would select one or two sons to go. These sons were selected because they seemed, in their parents' judgement, most likely to succeed academically. Daughters were rarely selected to go to school. Families who had very limited resources had to invest them wisely; investing in a girl's future earning potential would benefit the in-laws, not the birth parents.

Those children selected to go to school would be expected to devote the majority of their time to excelling scholastically. Students were treated with respect and were given many special privileges within their families. In general, students were expected only to study hard and to pass their exams. Other family members would take on the students' share of chores, family responsibilities and economic burden. Within the Hmong community at large, students were admired and coveted as future sons or daughters-in-law. Hmong parents who invested in their children's education hoped that these students would eventually be able to qualify for, take, and pass the civil service exams and thus become employed in high status government jobs.

The children who did not go to school remained close to their parents. They continued to follow their parents to and from the fields, hunting, fishing, and gardening. As they grew to be between ten and twelve, the children would take on a few more responsibilities. Boys would help with such things as the heavy field work and feeding and caring for the farm animals. Girls would begin cooking simple meals, help with the vegetable garden and do needlework. By the time children reached their teens, most knew at least basic living skills and were ready to start their own lives.

Marriage age for most Hmong was very young compared to modern-day Western standards. Most Hmong parents hoped to see each of their children married and started upon their own lives before dying. Since life spans were short in Laos, children were encouraged to marry early. Marriage age for girls was between 13 and 17 and for boys between 15 and 20. Sons were expected to bring their wives home to live in their parents' home until they had had one or two children. At that point, the couple would be permitted to build a residence of their own on a nearby plot. By the time he reached the age of 35 or so, many of the responsibilities of head of household for the family would be transferred to the oldest or most educated son. At this time the parents would go into semi-retirement.

Physical disciplinary measures were considered acceptable in Hmong society. Children were spanked when necessary and scolded by both parents. However, because of the strong emphasis on family ties in the Hmong culture, grudges were almost never held. Within a few minutes, or a day at the most, peace would return to the household after even the most severe physical punishment. Offenses considered serious enough to justify a spanking included disobedience to parents, unwillingness to help with chores, fighting with siblings, breaking utensils, and so on.

Since many Hmong parents knew very little about formal school

Implications for Educators:

❖For girls to be told at school that they can aspire to be doctors, astronauts, or even able to support themselves without husbands, and then to go home and enter the world in which the women's roles are so different, is perhaps one of the most far-reaching "new ideas" confronting the Hmong society as a whole.

❖American parents push children to independence and individual competition from the earliest ages. Hmong babies are held or carried; American babies are put in strollers, infant seats, and sleep alone in a crib. Crying is considered healthy in American children; Hmong children are seldom allowed to cry themselves to sleep. Americans pay close attention to developmental time tables; Hmong parents assume that "time will take care of it", whether toileting, reading, deafness, or tantrum throwing.

❖Hmong parents expect children to repay the debt of having been born and cared for; American parents invest great energy and money in insuring that children have a better life than they themselves had. Hmong parents make decisions to move, for example, based on the needs of the adults or the lineage group as a whole, where American middle class parents decide where to live based on the area schools' reputations. Hmong parents expect children to grow up, and later in life to "be like the others." American parents nourish children early in life to guarantee later competitive success as individuals.

❖Hmong children spend most of their free time in the company of other children, siblings and clanmates. American children spend more time in the company of adults, and expect they have the individual rights of adults from the earliest ages.

❖There is no real difference in the degree of physical punishment. In fact, Hmong children are often corrected quietly, without the humiliation of public chastisement. However, there are cases in which children who do not respond to either modeling by other children or quiet correction are spanked hard, often with a switch ("getting an eel"). These cases are really no different from American children who are spanked for a major violation of rules; in both cases, parents are liable for reporting to Child Protective Services under current California practices, if spanking is thought to be excessive. Schools can provide a valuable service by 1) explaining clearly to parents the differences between discipline and abuse; and 2) intervening with a bilingual paraprofessional to understand clearly the circumstances before suspected abuse is reported.

There are still cases in which school personnel interpret bruises or scratches on the child's skin as signs of abuse, rather than remnants of traditional folk remedies. Schools can provide personnel with cultural awareness presentations, and can send bilingual paraprofessionals to intervene.

❖School personnel should keep in mind that animists believe that it's dangerous for a child's spirit to be scared away; if the spirits are not called back with special ceremonies, the child might become sick or die. Various activities in school may cause the child's spirit to be scared away: encountering a big dog; looking at a green tomato worm in science class; touching a snake; having an accident on the playground or coming near death... .

ing systems, many did not keep abreast of their children's progress at school. Thus, there was rarely any disciplinary action taken with students who did not do well scholastically. Those children unable to continue to higher levels were scolded by their parents briefly, then returned to their previous lifestyle of helping around the farm.

❖Formal Education in Laos

Prior to the 1850's, the only formal education available in Laos was that found in the Buddhist temples (Berval, 1959). This was available only to limited numbers of males. Hmong children were generally not sent to Buddhist temples to receive their education. This was due to differences in religious beliefs between the Hmong and Lao. Hmong follow traditional beliefs based on a combination of ancestor worship and animism or have converted to Christianity, while most Lao are Buddhists. Another reason Hmong children did not attend Buddhist temples was that Buddhist temples, supported by Lao villages or towns, were usually not in close proximity to the mountain villages of the Hmong.

Under French domination, starting around the middle of the nineteenth century, secular schooling began to grow and eventually predominated (Roberts et al., 1966). Due to limitations such as lack of teachers, school buildings, and school supplies, education was available to only a few.

It was in 1939 that the first village school for Hmong children was established in Nong Het, an area inhabited by Hmong people and located in the northern part of Laos. It offered a beginning class and involved nine students. Before that date, a few privileged Hmong children had gone to Xieng Khouang City, the provincial capital, or to Vinh, in Central Vietnam, to receive a formal education.

After World War II, in response to pressure from the Hmong leaders of Xieng Khouang plateau, the schooling system started to extend to other Hmong-inhabited mountainous areas of Xieng Khouang province. An increasing number of the Hmong youth began to move from their traditional school of nature to an academic system of education. In 1960, the number of students totaled 1,500 in 20 village schools. In 1969, there were 10,000 students, distributed in seven elementary school units and more than 100 village schools, overseen by 450 teachers, of whom the majority were Hmong. About 50% of Hmong children of school age attended these village schools, established in the south of the Plain of Jars in Xieng Khouang province, in October 1969. Progressively, the elementary education system extended to other Hmong villages in other provinces in North Laos, where the schooling rate among the Hmong children had remained generally very low, close to zero. In 1971, Hmong educational progress was evidenced by the presence of 340 Hmong students at the high school level in France, the United States, Canada, and Australia. And the number of Hmong students continued to increase until the takeover of Laos by the Pathet Lao in 1975.

Once in school, the students began to learn how to deal with the Lao alphabet and the Lao language, required for their elementary education. It generally took them two or three years before they were able to write and to speak correctly this second language. Then they studied mathematics, social sciences, ethical behavior, and French; the latter was absolutely necessary to enter high school, which was conducted almost entirely in French and generally offered in the cities, far away from Hmong villages.

Implications for Educators:

When hiring bilingual aides, keep in mind this background. If the aides had up to three years of school in Laos, then they probably can read and write Lao. Aides who are required to translate for the sciences, government, history, or higher level math would need to have had 4-6 years, or more, of school. Even with that background, translating without adequate dictionaries will be difficult. Young adults probably had neither Lao schooling nor sufficient American education to allow them to translate for junior high or senior high classes. A better alternative is to find an older adult, who had more than three years of Lao schooling, but whose English may not be as clearly spoken as younger Hmong. The primary purpose of bilingual aides is to reteach concepts in the primary language.

Only a very small number of Hmong children were able to attend schools recognized and supported by the Royal Lao government. Reasons for this were manifold and various. A major cause of low attendance of Hmong children in schools was that along with Buddhist schools, these schools were also located far away, meaning the Hmong family would have had to be able to pay for room and board for each student. Secondarily, most Hmong families supported themselves by subsistence farming. In such an economy the child's labor could not easily be spared by the family. Another reason why relatively small numbers of Hmong students succeeded in passing through the formal education system was that it was difficult for Hmong children to compete with the predominantly Lao students and overcome the language and cultural barriers. Hmong students had to be extremely patient and persevering to pass and to excel in the Lao and French schools. Only the wealthier Hmong families could afford to send their children to low-land schools, and usually for only three or four years.

Implications for Educators:

Hmong have been a minority group throughout history, and many of the proverbs and adages teach how to get along successfully with the majority group, while maintaining Hmong independence and identity.

During the decade prior to 1975, a number of private schools not officially recognized by the government appeared and offered curricula taught in Lao, French, English, and Chinese. Some of the better educated Hmong adults now in the U.S. attended Catholic Schools run by French missionaries. Young men would attend schools such as these in hope of being prepared to take civil service or military entrance exams. However, again, only the wealthy could afford to educate their children in this way.

During the period of American involvement in Laos, General Vang Pao assigned some of the officers to become teachers. He would send them out to Hmong villages and there they would set up a little hut and call it a school. It was not mandatory, but, if a family wanted to and could afford to, they could send their children there. These were not accredited schools, nor were they voluntary activities, because a soldier could get more pay by becoming a teacher. These schools were taught in Lao, even though the teachers were Hmong.

In Laos, prior to 1975, graduates of the nationally recognized schooling system were assured civil service jobs by the government. The level of the job and the pay scale were dependent upon which certificate or diploma had been achieved. Thus, those with tenth grade diplomas received higher pay than those with sixth grade certificates, and those with high school diplomas received even more. No matter what level of work, the Hmong traditionally regarded any government employee as having very high social status.

Little is known about changes in the educational system in Laos under the Communist government after 1975. It is reported that the system of grade levels has changed. First through sixth grades remain the same, followed by a secondary sequence of seventh through tenth grades. There is a strong emphasis on technical schooling. The eleventh to thirteenth grades have been eliminated.

❖Typical School Day for a Hmong Child

Most schools in Laos began instruction at 8:00 in the morning. After about two hours, a fifteen-minute recess was given. Then classes resumed until noon. A one-and-a-half or two-hour period was given for lunch, before classes resumed at 1:30 or 2:00 p.m. Classes then continued until 5:00 p.m. with another 15-minute recess at mid-afternoon. For Hmong students, this meant a very long day. Since most Hmong villages were located several miles outside of town, and there were no buses or public transportation, Hmong students would have to rise very early in the morning, often as early as 4:00 or 4:30 a.m. Most Hmong mothers would also get up at that time and cook a quick breakfast for their children. The mothers would also prepare and pack lunches for their children. The children would then join other students walking into town. Many would have to walk from three to ten miles to get to their schools. In the early morning it was often still very dark, and the children would carry little "torches," which were really sticks cut from a special type of pine or bamboo tree.

Upon arriving at school, students would play in the school yard until the warning bell rang. The students would then line up outside the door of the schoolhouse. At the teachers' signal, the students would quietly walk in and stand by their assigned seats. They would wait for their teacher to signal that they were permitted to sit down. Then lessons would start for the day.

Teachers were accorded very high status in Laos, and students were expected to show them every respect. When passing the teacher, students would clasp their hands in front of their faces as a gesture of respect. Few students dared to raise their hands to ask questions when a teacher lectured. Most students simply did their best to memorize their texts, which was the standard approach to learning in Laos.

Teachers were allowed to discipline their students in whatever way they saw fit. It was not uncommon for teachers to take a stick and hit a child's hands or legs if they had not completed their lessons or were caught whispering or fidgeting in class. At other times they would ask the student with the highest grades to do the actual beating for them.

When it was time for recess or lunch break, students would again rise and stand by their seats waiting for permission to leave the room. While most of the town children would return to their homes for lunch, Hmong students would eat the lunches brought from home in the school yard.

At the end of the school day, Hmong student would again gather for the long walk home. They would often arrive back in the village between 6:30 and 8:00 p.m. They would eat dinner with their families and then have to do their homework. Since Hmong villages did not have electricity, students would study by "torch light" or light from the fireplace. Torches for studying were made by stringing together a certain type of oily nut. Hmong students would have to study long hours as they were memorizing texts in a second language, either Lao or French. By the time homework was completed, it was usually time to go to sleep as the next morning would mean another early rising.

❖Education During the Relocation Period in Laos

The education described above may have been typical of Hmong who are now in mid-adulthood, and of younger Hmong whose villages were so isolated that the events of the war did not disrupt their lives until the late 1960's or even the early 1970's. Smalley (1986) describes the rapid changes in lifestyle that occurred during the *Laos resettlement* stage. During this period of time, Hmong were relocated into large refugee settlements, where they mingled with many different ethnic groups, were separated from husbands and brothers who fought in the army, and depended on economic aid for survival. Despite all the turmoil and disruption during this period, living in large settlements enabled more children to attend school, and presented the Hmong with challenges to the past traditional practices. Many coped with the changes only with great difficulty, while others adapted more creatively, learning new skills and adopting non-traditional lifestyles.

Thus, it is difficult to speak of traditional experiences that apply to the present generation of children and their parents; their lives were already radically different from the days of the isolated villages before they left Laos.

❖Languages & Literacy in Laos

There is currently little information available on the literacy rates in Laos. Even if there were, it would not accurately reflect the literacy rates of the Hmong who lived in the mountainous rural areas of Laos and therefore did not have the opportunity to attend Laotian schools.

One study that has been conducted in the U.S. included interviews about past educational experiences and levels of literacy. Reder (1982) reports on a survey of about 2,700 Hmong adults in a West Coast community. The majority (62%) of those interviewed were from Luang Prabang and Sayaboury provinces in Laos. Reder's survey found 73% of the individuals had never attended school, and 12% had one to three years of school; 7% had four to six years; 1% had seven to eight years, and another 1% had nine or more years. About half (48%) spoke no Lao, which corresponded closely to the percentage of the sample who were women (48%); 70% had no proficiency in reading Hmong; 82% had no proficiency in reading Lao (Green and Reder, 1986). The level of education of adult women was much lower than that of the men; 92% of the women and 46% of the men had had no formal education (Reder, 1982, p. 282).

Some scholars have indicated that the Hmong in Laos were, on the whole, a pre-literate people. In the sense that the Hmong did not have a written language of their own prior to the end of World War II when missionaries developed one using the Roman alphabet, this is true. Hmong has been an oral language only, but maintained as a distinct language for at least 4,000 years (Vang and Lewis, 1984). Prior to the present adult generation of Hmong, formal education was not an important aspect of the Hmong culture. But beginning with the present adult generation there has been a new emphasis on increasing opportunities for formal education, especially for young men. Thus, among successively lower age groups of Hmong, one is likely to find increasingly higher levels (at least among the men) of literacy in either Lao, English, or French.

Implications for Educators:

Community service agencies dealing with the Hmong population find that they can use Lao interpreters or Lao written translations for the adult men (mid-twenties to late forties), but for the young children and the old adults, they must use oral Hmong to communicate.

For the Hmong students who entered Lao schools after 1960, reading and writing Lao was studied throughout elementary school, from grades 1 through 6. In general, a person was considered literate in Lao after having completed a third or fourth grade education. Completion of a sixth grade education was considered the minimum level of achievement to enter such professions as primary teaching, nursing, and lower level government work and was highly coveted. Relatively much smaller numbers of students were able to continue to higher education, and obtaining a tenth grade certificate was considered a very notable achievement. Receiving a diploma after completing the thirteenth grade at a French lycee was even more prestigious.

Since the 1960's, it has been possible to study a variety of different foreign languages in the Lao schools. Most students studied French as a second language in elementary school in preparation for qualifying to enter high schools, which were taught in French. High school students were required to study an additional foreign language in order to qualify to obtain the *Brevet d'Etudes du Deuxieme Cycle* (high school diploma equivalent). Most schools offered a choice between English, Spanish, and Bali.

From the 1960's until 1975, English was used more and more in the military, education and business circles, and more and more students chose to study English to meet their foreign language requirement. Private non-accredited schools also began offering English lessons at that time for those who had aspirations for becoming employed by the American military or American businesses.

Communication between the Hmong army and American personnel was necessary because the Hmong and Americans were allies in fighting the secret war. Few Americans spoke Lao or Hmong, necessitating the use of English. Many Hmong soldiers attended intensive English courses from three to six months long in order to take such jobs as air traffic control officers, radio operators, and pilots. It was mainly officers who were sent to English-language schools. The emphasis was on oral skills, but there was some instruction in reading and report writing. Some Hmong picked up the language informally through their association with the American military. A few were sent to schools in America.[2]

As more and more Americans were seen in Lao cities, businesses and services sprang up to serve their needs. Those who wished to cater to Americans of course quickly learned to speak their language. Restaurants, tailors, general merchandise stores, laundries, maids, gardeners, and many others found it lucrative at that time to be able to communicate in English.

During this time period, Laos was the recipient of a great deal of American aid, and through contact of these agencies which provided services such as economic development projects, urban development projects, and teaching projects, others also came in contact with the English language and culture. Nevertheless, few of the Hmong who eventually came to the U.S. as refugees had more than slight acquaintance with the English language while in Laos.

---

[2] For more on how Hmong men have acquired English literacy, see Malcolm, 1983.

Contact with the English language and culture continued for the Hmong in Thai refugee camps. At first there were only a few English classes in the camps, organized by the refugees themselves. There was room in these classes for only a fraction of those interested in learning English. Later classes were set up in which English was taught by Thai instructors assisted by Americans. Beginning in 1980, English classes were made mandatory for at least heads-of-household prior to resettlement in the United States. Many of the top camp administrators, medical personnel, and immigration officers, and so on were Americans, and thus camp residents came in contact with English-speaking persons.

The relatively few Hmong who learned to read and write in any of these ways in Laos obtained literacy in Lao, French, or English. But since there was no formal training available in the Hmong language, none achieved Hmong literacy by these means. Many of the Hmong who are literate in Lao learned to write Hmong only after fleeing Laos to refugee camps in Thailand. Thus it is not uncommon to see a man reading notes written in Lao, speaking in English, and presumably thinking in Hmong.

❖Value Placed on Literacy Skills

In general, it is safe to say that the Hmong culture places a very high value on obtaining education, and literacy, for its children. It is considered very desirable by both young and old. But two problems exist with regards to their positive attitude about literacy. First of all, it is generally not literacy in Hmong but in another language that they find desirable. Second, whether in Laos or in the United States, Hmong parents do not have the experience of being a student. They do not personally know the behaviors required for their children to be successful and continue beyond two or three years of school.

Factors in Refugee Camps

❖Refugee Camps in Thailand

Hmong refugees, after crossing the Laos/Thailand border, have generally entered one of several refugee camps in northeastern Thailand. Refugee camps have appeared and disappeared over the past ten years, according to the prevailing international policies, and local Thai priorities. Almost all have remained in these camps for a year or two—in some cases many years—prior to qualifying for resettlement.

When the Hmong people fled their country to go to Thailand, one of their preoccupations was how to continue to provide their children with education in the refugee camps. In Namphong, as well as in many other Hmong refugee centers, many educated young people offered themselves as teachers without salary to their younger companions. These were the students at the *Lycee de Vientiane*, a Lao-French high school, or former teacher trainees at Sisavangvong University in Dongdock. Because there was no school in the camp when they arrived in 1975, these volunteer teachers had their young students sitting in the yard, in the shade of a tree. They organized the first schooling program according to the ages, educational backgrounds and needs of the students. They generally taught Hmong to those who never had the opportunity to go to school, French to those who were preparing themselves to go to France, and English to those who were planning to come to the United States.

After the Namphong Center population had been transferred to Ban Vinai in 1976, World Vision, a voluntary organization, took over the Hmong education. A former director of the educational program explained the situation:

> *In 1979, there were three school units in Ban Vinai where 31,300 Hmong refugees lived. Each school unit included three or four buildings which comprised six classrooms each. The program involved 66 full time Hmong teachers and 2,000 Hmong students from grades one to four in the Thai educational system, equivalent to grades 1 through 5 in the American school system. The teaching was only done in Thai. Therefore, the students had to learn how to read and how to count in Thai, following the Thai program of education. World Vision took charge of the construction of buildings, provided schools with books and supplies, and granted symbolic salaries to the teachers.*

The Royal Thai Government constructed an additional school unit in Ban Vinai, staffed by more than ten Thai teachers. This contribution was very helpful and appreciated by the Hmong refugees, whose numbers increased every day. Finally, *Ecoles sans Frontières*, a French private organization, took a role in Hmong education by adding two hours a day of French in the program, and involving seven young Hmong teachers and 250 Hmong students.[3]

The Nongkhai camp was only two acres in size, but this refugee center welcomed more than 10,500 Hmong in March, 1976. The crowding (one person per square meter) and the hot tropical weather favored the development of disease, and provoked a very high mortality—close to 33 per thousand. Children under twelve years old, who constituted 45 per cent of this population, suffered the most.

It was in this atmosphere that education was developed in Nongkhai. It started with twelve volunteer teachers–eleven Hmong and one Lao–and about 200 Hmong students (six to fourteen years old). Their "school" was constructed of pieces of wood, covered with large pieces of black plastic, with no walls. The Thai Catholic Charities came to take over the Hmong education in Nongkhai in December, 1976. Six Catholic sisters recruited fifteen Hmong teachers for a three-month period of training. When these men were able to read, write, and speak Thai correctly, they were employed to teach the Hmong children in the camp. The Thai Catholic Charities undertook the construction of four school buildings. Each building included six classrooms. About 1,000 Hmong children were involved in a four-year program (grades 1 through 4) under the supervision of the Catholic sisters. They learned the Thai language, studied the history of Thailand, discovered the sciences, received Christian instruction, and learned the Hmong writing system.

Later on, after the Royal Thai Government had transferred the Nongkhai Hmong refugee population to Ban Vinai in July, 1979, the United Nations High Commissioner for Refugees (UNHCR) took over the Hmong education in the camp. As of 1987, each of the camp's nine centers has a school for grades one through three and there is one kindergarten for the camp. There is now one educational facility for 1,300 children, grades four through six. School attendance, up to age

---

[3]Information obtained by Dao Yang from the former director of the educational program in Ban Vinai in 1978 and from his personal notes taken while in the refugee camps in Thailand.

fourteen, involves 7,300 children, being taught by 50 Thai teachers and approximately 300 Hmong teachers. There are teaching facilities for mentally retarded children and for deaf or blind persons. About 1,000 people are also involved in adult literacy programs. Finally, some vocational programs have been organized and include typing, sewing, mechanics, blacksmithing, carpentry, barbering, and bicycle and typewriter repair.

❖Phanat Nikhom Transit Center

After being accepted for resettlement to the United States, Hmong families are moved to Phanat Nikhom, a transitional camp near Bangkok. There, most stay a minimum of six additional months prior to actual entry into the United States. During this time, attendance in a six-month English class and American Cultural Orientation is required. Run by an organization called the Consortium, Phanat Nikhom provides English, cultural orientation and work orientation training. The goal is to help adult refugees acquire language skills, and to prepare them to adjust to American life.

English classes are offered at six different levels. Level 1 is for those who speak no English at all, while the highest level, level 6, is for those able to communicate fairly well in English. Those refugees who only complete level 1 prior to entry into the United States are only able to speak a few common English phrases; while those who have completed level 6 are fairly fluent in English. The majority of refugees have completed levels 2 or 3 before entering the United States, and this means that they are able to communicate at least a little with their American sponsors, case managers, and social workers. Since 1983, the English level that each refugee has achieved is printed on the back of the immigration and naturalization document that he or she brings to the U.S.

A special program, called the PASS program (Preparation for American Secondary Schools), has been established for young refugees who will enter junior or senior high schools in the United States. The content is ESL, math and American studies.

The American Culture Orientation course is intensive and covers many aspects of life in the United States. Use of and maintenance of American plumbing, large and small appliances, and electrical facilities is covered. Also covered are how to shop for, store and prepare American foods; American holidays; the school system; business and work ethics; American etiquette; and many other aspects of the American culture.

Factors in California

❖Parents' Attitude Towards Education

Hmong parents always consider education as a key to the future of their children. Back in Laos, they admired educated people and wanted their children to take part in the development of their own community and of the country as a whole. But war and poverty did not allow them to realize their dream. As refugees in the United States, they are still worried about their children's future. Transferred directly from the mountains of northern Laos to the industrial cities and towns of America, the Hmong youth encounter many problems and difficulties in their process of adjustment to the American system of education. First of all, they have to face a linguistic barrier which prevents them from learning with maximum efficiency and, along the way, developing their intellectual faculties. Second, many of them came to this country with a weak background in the sciences (math, physics, chemistry, biology), because their studies in Laos were interrupted over and over by the war which destroyed their villages and their schools (where there were any), and by their long stay in the refugee camps in Thailand, where literacy instruction, dictionaries, and so on, were generally not available. Thus, they have a hard time keeping up with American classmates in this country. Finally, many of the Hmong young people drop out of class before finishing their high school education. Only a very small number are able to continue their studies at the university level and obtain a diploma or an advanced degree.

Today, children make up more than 50% of the Hmong population in the United States. Tomorrow, these children will be its leaders to a new life. At present, Hmong children need help to prepare themselves to be able to bear such a responsibility. Too young to identify completely with the old world or to be completely and unselfconsciously identified with the new, Hmong adolescents constantly live with frustration. Too early uprooted from their own society, Hmong children do not know their own culture well and sometimes adopt the behavior of the American children. Some Hmong families experience generational conflicts and some parents experience marital problems because of the divergence of views about how they should live their lives in this country. In this kind of environment some children do not learn Hmong as well as their parents would like, while at the same time they are not completely proficient in English.

Implications for Educators:

One of the major handicaps that older Hmong students face is the lack of adequate materials to support their study, especially in the sciences. Vietnamese and Chinese students can find many dictionaries, which are drawn from a well-formulated body of formal knowledge, or they can find educated individuals in the community to explain difficult concepts. For example, how can an aide translate or explain *cell* in a way that helps understanding in science, when there's no corresponding concept in Hmong? *Cell* may be translated in any number of ways, including *a little piece.* Now, imagine how to explain *DNA, mitosis, meiosis.* How does an aide explain the process of genetic determination of traits, mutations, or the fact that two X chromosomes result in a female, but one X and one Y results in a male? It requires teaching concepts that American-born students learn over a period of time. It requires teaching concepts that differ from commonly held beliefs (in this case that the mother determines the sex of the offspring). Teachers can help the process by rewriting the essential concepts in straightforward English, for the bilingual aide to use when explaining and relating the new concepts to existing concepts. The state framework for science lists the key concepts taught from kindergarten to grade 12, and can be used to fill in the gaps for students entering American education mid-stream. If you have a Hmong paraprofessionals who have had science training in Laos beyond the 5th or 6th year of school, then they could use the framework to give a "crash course" to newly arrived junior high and senior high students, teaching basic vocabulary and concepts from usually taught from kindergarten to grade 6 or grade 9. Social studies is less of a problem area, because it is generally a study of people and events (easier to translate).

Most Hmong families are very concerned about the situation of Hmong youth in this country. They are aware that the competition in the job market in the next few years will be very difficult. Those young people who do not have a good education may not be able to find a good job and to build a better future. Many people think that it is necessary to develop Hmong teachers who will participate in teaching Hmong children, who will be able to involve the Hmong families more effectively in the American system of education, and who will work closely with the school districts in planning for the education of Hmong children and youth, providing role models from the Hmong community. At the same time teachers who are not Hmong but who are aware of the backgrounds of these students and the conflicts they face can also help Hmong children to surmount the obstacles in their paths.

Already there are examples of outstanding success among Hmong youths. Pahoua Yang, graduating from a Wisconsin senior high school, gained first place in a statewide contest for scholarship and was

---

Implications for Educators:

In the absence of certificated Hmong teachers, districts can fill the gap in other ways. The key to a good program is hiring the right person to act as the "bridge" between parents and teachers, between Hmong and English, between the old world and the new one. Hiring the right person means creating positions with new titles, unique qualifications, flexible job descriptions, and pay adequate to provide for long-term employment. The Hmong community in most cities is organized, and the elders and younger bilingual adults who are respected can be involved in the search for the right person. Involving the community leadership helps the district find a person who has credibility with the community; parents will be more willing to participate and consider his opinions during conflicts or misunderstandings.

---

honored by President Ronald Reagan at the White House in February, 1986. Teng Christopher Thao of Minneapolis became the first Hmong to be graduated from an American law school when he received his law degree in 1986. Community groups often hold celebration and recognition ceremonies for those who obtain degrees—whether high school, adult education high school equivalency, Associate Arts, Bachelor's, Master's, or PhD's. *Haiv Hmoob,* a Hmong language magazine published in Minneapolis twice a year, lists the names of students enrolled in higher education across the country. The various clans take great pride in seeing how many of their members are becoming educated.

❖Parents' Attitudes about Involvement in Education

In the face of new social, cultural and economic problems in the United States, Hmong parents and other adults strongly encourage Hmong youth and children to study hard in school and to get as much education as possible in order to be better prepared for their future in this country. But this encouragement tends to be limited to good advice from the community leaders and some financial assistance from the parents. Because the majority of the Hmong are illiterate and speak little or no English, they are not able to check the school work and

Implications for Educators:

Teachers can help parents understand what their children are bringing home by using a consistent symbol, word or color of ink to indicate how well work has been done. Without a system, non-literate parents rely on other cues. For example, parents might be told that if there's a lot of writing by the teacher on the paper, then it's bad; if there's a short word, then it's good. If parents know when to expect a work folder from school, then they can ask to see it.

There's a great volume of written communication between the school and home, including advertisements and information about optional activities. If the information is important, teachers might mark a red X or other symbol on it; parents can then take that paper to be translated, rather than taking everything. If it's important information, teachers would be wise to have the bilingual aide call home and explain to the parents.

An important part of the parent education program is explaining grades, homework policy, and expectations of the school. *Support your child* is too vague; it might mean paying for food and rent while the student stays in school, rather than going to work. As part of a parent education program, school personnel should be able to explain clearly what they assume to be true for children in their classes. For example:

❖Children should get 8 hours of sleep, parents should see that they go to sleep early enough.

❖Children should either have food before school, or bring a snack to eat during the morning.

❖Children should be expected to do homework at a certain time each day.

❖Children should stay home when they're sick (explain what symptoms are considered sickness).

❖Parents should expect their children to learn, and do well.

❖Parents should take an active interest in their children's schooling; explain clearly what "active *interest*" means.

❖Parents should discipline their children, but not abuse them.

Parents will come to school for meetings and conferences, when they know that they will be able to understand what is said. There is usually a good "grapevine" in the community, and the Hmong paraprofessional should be able to get the word to the heads of household directly, and encourage them to come.

School personnel should resist the temptation to convince parents to do what the school wants. Many parents are suspicious of strong efforts to convince. A more effective technique is to have the trusted Hmong paraprofessional present the pros and the cons, cite other examples familiar to the parents, and even give his own personal opinion.....then wait for the parents to decide on their own. The school has to be willing to accept a negative answer, even in cases of special education placements, or other decisions they see as vital to the student.

Parent participation preschools are a good place to begin the process of involving Hmong parents in their child's education, and to demonstrate the value of primary language development along with early exposure to English.

monitor the academic progress of their children and to guide them in choosing vocational goals consonant with their abilities. Hmong parents are likely to trust their children and let them do what they want at home. They are ready to believe what the young people tell them about their homework, their grades and their activities in class. Moreover, Hmong parents generally think they should not criticize the American system of education, which they feel must have given rise to the evident American technical progress, high standards of living and modern ways of life. They are thus ready to entrust the education of their children to the teachers and the school. As a result, very few Hmong parents attend parent-teacher meetings or sign up for conferences. Teachers and other school officials therefore need to make special efforts to educate Hmong parents about their role in the public education of their children and to strongly encourage their active cooperation with the schools.

❖Availability of Trained Hmong Educators

In 1987, about 13,000 Hmong students attend California schools, from kindergarten through twelfth grade, with an unknown number studying in institutions of higher education. However, only a very small number of Hmong teachers are currently involved in the American system of education. When they arrived in the United States, some of them took the first employment offered in order to survive; others could not teach because of their lack of English proficiency; still others were employed part-time as teacher aides but later quit the job when they found it did not pay enough to meet family needs. Many decided to change occupations. After undertaking a short-term course of training, they started to work wherever they could find a job as machinists, electricians, plumbers, mechanics, or in other vocations not requiring high levels of English proficiency.

❖Value Placed on Hmong Language Instruction

In the United States as more and more Hmong children enter the public schools and adults learn English as a second language through various programs, the Hmong are slowly becoming literate not only in English but in Hmong as well. Since the Hmong language currently uses roman characters, very soon after becoming familiar with the English alphabet and the sounds the letters represent, most Hmong students learn to read and write Hmong. Thus, teachers may find that many Hmong who are at the third or fourth grade level are able to read and write simple Hmong. Most Hmong children aged 10 and younger do not show much interest in learning Hmong, and only when they reach their teens, when for example they begin to write love letters to other Hmong teenagers, do they begin to have an interest in learning to read and write the Hmong language.

In past generations there was little opportunity or reason for Hmong individuals to use their Hmong writing skills. In the United States there are a few newsletters and/or collections of short stories and poems which are circulated within some Hmong communities from time to time. Many of these are written in Hmong and this provides an opportunity for individuals to write and submit articles. Other than this, Hmong reading and writing is most commonly used to communicate by means of letters to friends and family members in other cities or countries. Recently, creating modern Hmong poems and setting them to Western or Chinese music has become popular among some Hmong teen groups. Christian Hmong regularly read hymnals and the Bible.

The majority of Hmong elders and adults support maintenance of the Hmong language and culture but feel they are unable to enforce this view on their children. Coming from a multilingual society, most know the value of being biliterate and bicultural, but if forced to choose one or the other, most agree that knowing English well is the priority, essential for success in America.

❖Community Resources for Hmong Language Development

In traditional Hmong society there were several mechanisms which encouraged youngsters to know about the Hmong culture and expand their knowledge of the Hmong language. These mechanisms are still working to varying extents amongst the Hmong refugee community.

One mechanism still fairly commonly encountered in the Hmong communities is the telling of stories and legends. Grandparents, although more commonly the grandmothers, often spend several hours a week entertaining and teaching their children and grandchildren with Hmong stories and legends that have been passed by work of mouth for generations. In this way, Hmong youngsters learn much about their heritage, traditions, and language.

The learning of Hmong songs, which in reality means Hmong poems, is another way in which Hmong youth become well versed in their language. Hmong songs are an integral part of the Hmong culture, being involved in the courtship, wedding, religious, ceremonial, and funeral processes. From the time that children begin to talk, they hear their older siblings practice singing and making up new songs and rhymes. Mothers and grandmothers also spend much of their spare time teaching children how to sing and make rhymes. Teens who are skilled at making clever rhymes soon gain popularity among their peers. All this encourages Hmong youth in general to practice this art. Memorizing song patterns and developing the creativity to construct new rhymes expands the vocabulary and knowledge of the Hmong language among the Hmong youth.

Another way that Hmong elders teach their children more about the Hmong language is through the teaching of traditional ceremonies and rituals. Each ceremony and ritual is accompanied by certain songs and verses. As young boys reach the age of ten or so, they are encouraged by their male elders to first observe, then take part in, then officiate at various ceremonies and rituals. Through this type of experience, the teen boys learn the traditions they will need to know how to establish their own households, and also learn more about the Hmong language.

❖Community Resources for Teaching Hmong Literacy

While past generations did not have the resources or the means to learn to read and write Hmong, the present California Hmong community is the first group of Hmong to be able to do so. Outside of Southern China, Laos, and Ban Vinai refugee camp, California perhaps has the highest concentration of Hmong residents in the world. Hmong, in general, prefer to live together in sizable communities in order to be better able to reestablish traditional community support systems. However, there are presently no formal systems existing in the Hmong community to provide Hmong language instruction. Reasons for this may be lack of past experience in establishing a schooling system, lack of financial support, and lack of accredited teaching personnel.

However, on an informal basis, Hmong language instruction is being actively pursued in the California Hmong community. Hmong community leaders estimate that 75% of those Hmong who learn the alphabet now know how to read and write Hmong, but this estimate may be too optimistic. If this were true it would mean that most men and women below the age of 65 (those above 65 are not required to attend ESL classes) down to Hmong teens have a basic knowledge of reading and writing Hmong. Long-term residents of refugee camps are more likely to be literate in Hmong than short-term residents, the reason being that they don't have very much to do, and they aren't being forced to learn English, and they therefore learn to write Hmong in order to be able to communicate with their relatives in that way. Those who spend less time in refugee camps come to the U.S. quickly and then learn English rather than Hmong.

Implications for educators:

Reading and writing Hmong is fairly simple once the alphabet and coding systems are learned. However, reading quickly, with fluency and immediate sight word recognition is a higher level of reading that is not usually differentiated when responding to the question, *Do you read and write Hmong?* In other words, the process of reading is decoding each word, pronouncing it loud enough to hear, and then identifying what that word is, by hearing it. Writing Hmong is a reverse process; encoding initial consonants, vowel, and tone. This, along with the lack of consistent standards for spelling regional differences in pronunciation, and lack of good dictionaries, cause Hmong readers difficulty when reading quickly for main ideas or proof-reading written work.

When schools have translations prepared, it's a good idea to first write it in simple, straightforward English, then have it translated into Hmong. Another Hmong should read and translate it back to English, to see if the idea has been adequately communicated. Finally, have one or two others proof-read the text for accuracy of encoding. Common errors include transposition of *ia* and *ai, ua* and *au,* and confusions between *r* and *ts, a* and *aa, dl* and *d,* which represent differences between White and Green Hmong pronunciations, and different ways of assigning tones.

Instruction in reading Hmong is usually done on a one-to-one basis, with individuals learning from a friend or a relative who has learned to read and write Hmong from another friend or relative. It is the general consensus of those who know how to read and write Hmong, that if one already knows the alphabet and the Hmong language, it takes less than a week of instruction to be able to read and write Hmong. It can only be concluded that the attitude of the Hmong community towards Hmong language instruction is very positive, with the majority of the Hmong community actively seeking it. Whether the Hmong communities will move towards formalizing instruction remains to be seen.

While there are no institutions either in Laos or in California involved in encouraging Hmong children's language development per se, various Christian religious groups have made significant contributions to the preservation and development of the Hmong language. The most commonly used method of writing Hmong, using the roman alphabet, was developed by missionaries in Laos. Religious scholars have also translated the Bible and many hymns into the Hmong language (The Bible Society of Thailand, 1980 and Vang, 1983) Hmong Christian groups thus read and sing Hmong songs during every service they attend, and this also helps in encouraging Hmong literacy.

Several agencies have been involved in the preservation of the Hmong language. Examples are the Center for Applied Linguistics in

Implications for educators:

Schools can play an important role in helping the Hmong community maintain the language and culture. Teachers do not need to worry that the children will not learn English; the teachings of the society emphasize knowing the majority language well. However, teachers can acknowledge the importance of knowing how to read and write Hmong, and can encourage efforts in a variety of ways, other than full bilingual classroom programs.

❖After third or fourth grade, have the students write the reading vocabulary words in Hmong as well as English. Have the bilingual aide go over the reading vocabulary and key concepts in Hmong. If the Hmong children are shy about using Hmong in front of other classmates, provide a time and place for review or reteaching in Hmong; it's important not to use art or physical education time for this, as the students don't want to miss class activities.

❖Set up a homework program in which older siblings use the Hmong equivalents of basic word lists, like the Dolch Basic 220 word list, to tutor younger siblings on a regular basis.

❖Encourage the recording of Hmong oral lore, in Hmong and translated into English.

❖Involve the non-Hmong students in learning simple Hmong words.

❖Help set up Hmong literacy classes through the local recreation program for summer vacation and after school; offer Hmong literacy during summer school programs; assist the Hmong community organization set up classes at school sites.

❖Keep in mind that until there are useable Hmong dictionaries, secondary students may not see much value in learning Hmong. Demonstrate ways to use Hmong to help learn English material: taking notes, writing equivalent words, noting pronunciation, etc. Help the librarian locate Hmong language books for the community and school libraries.

❖Above all, the teacher is a model to the students, Hmong and non-Hmong. Many communities have programs that introduce "survival Hmong" to non-Hmong. In addition to learning a few words, the teacher is better able to understand and anticipate problem areas in class, and learns a great deal of the culture via study of the language. For example, when the teacher of the survival Hmong class has difficulty in finding a direct translation for *sister*, or *proud*, *volunteer* or *intelligent*, it's an indication that the two societies have different concepts that underlie the vocabulary.

Washington, DC, which has produced an *English-Hmong Phrasebook* (Thao, 1981), Cornell University in New York which has published a *White Hmong-English Dictionary* (Heimbach, 1969), and the Zellerbach Family Fund which has supported the bilingual collection of Hmong legends, entitled *Grandmother's Path, Grandfather's Way* (Vang and Lewis, 1984). Yves Bertrais, in French Guiana, has trained Hmong assistants to transcribe and type into a computer the Hmong oral works he has recorded over the past thirty years; they have completed several Hmong texts, and continue to work on others in the *Patrimoine Culturel Hmong* collection. An Australian novelist, Nyiajpov Lis, has written several novels in Hmong. Two periodicals, *Haiv Hmoob* (written entirely in Hmong) and *The Hmong World* (written in Hmong and English), are being published in this country. The publication of these types of bilingual and monolingual works is providing much needed resources for Hmong youth in their quest for literacy in their own language. (See the Bibliography for additional bilingual and monolingual Hmong works.)

❖Use of Hmong in the Community

The Hmong language is used and heard at the majority of Hmong community events, such as mutual assistance association meetings, church services, and various social events. Although certain English phrases may occasionally be inserted during discussions—usually phrases which refer to American ideas which cannot be translated into Hmong—almost all communications between Hmong adults are conducted in the Hmong language. At Hmong parties, weddings, christenings, and funerals the majority of people are heard speaking Hmong. Even in Oriental stores, or other places where Hmong families might meet each other, Hmong is the predominant language spoken.

Hmong is still spoken as a first language in the majority of Hmong homes at the present time. A primary reason for this is that most elders and adults are not yet, and may never be, fluent in the English language. Thus, preschool children, adults, and elders use Hmong almost exclusively as their language for communication. As the children grow up and enter the American school system, it becomes increasingly common to hear them communicate with each other in English. For children who have grown up in the United States, after a few years in school, it seems that many have become more comfortable communicating in English. As time passes, it seems that more and more children use Hmong only when communicating with elders, and if given a preference, will use English instead.

❖Use of English in the Community

Most of the refugees who arrived between 1975 and 1977 had American sponsors. Either individual families or churches were the common sponsors during that time period. Thus, refugee families arriving then immediately came into contact with English. Often, there were difficulties in communication between sponsors and refugees at the initial contact, but usually within a few months the head-of-household would be able to speak at least some broken English. For those Hmong who have moved away from their sponsors to live near relatives, or whose sponsors have not kept in touch after the first few weeks or months, of course, these contacts have now been lost.

After 1977, many Hmong refugees were sponsored by other Hmong families who had already resettled in the United States. However, refugees are still processed by one of the national voluntary agencies, and each refugee family is usually assigned to a case worker and/or case manager who follows them for the first few months of resettlement. Interviews with the case manager, mandatory health screening, and other interviews with job counselors and welfare workers are common contacts refugee families have with American personnel.

The majority of Hmong refugees live in apartments or low cost houses, and of course have contact with American neighbors. Often, although Hmong is spoken exclusively in many Hmong homes, preschool children become semi-fluent in English by playing with neighborhood children. Those who have older siblings who learn English in schools also pick up the language from hearing these siblings speak and play.

Some Hmong families who have converted to Christian religions have additional contact with Americans through their churches. Also, there is daily contact with Americans at markets, shopping centers, and recreational areas. Another almost universal contact refugees have with the English language is through television, as almost every family soon owns a set. Children often pick up a great deal of idiomatic speech by watching cartoons and popular shows.

Some Hmong teens have begun patronizing local entertainment establishments and of course encounter American teens there. A few teens, as well as adults, have also begun finding employment and of course learn a great deal of English through talking with their co-workers and employers. On the job, Hmong learn oral skills, idiomatic meanings, and how to joke and socialize.

The English proficiency of Hmong parents varies widely. Those who have learned another language in addition to Hmong learn English more quickly; those who can read and write Hmong learn more English. Persons who can't read or write learn only what they hear and remember. As their children grow up and speak more and more English at home, it is common to find many parents also picking up and using more English. Most are able to speak at least some basic English with their children, although many are more comfortable speaking in Hmong. It is becoming increasingly common to hear conversations between parents and children where the parents speak Hmong and the children answer in English, yet both understand each other. In general, it is safe to say that while relatively few Hmong parents are fluent in English, the majority know at least some survival English, and can usually communicate simple thoughts and ideas. Many also know, through hearing their children, numerous idiomatic phrases.

There is a wide range in the English language proficiency of Hmong adults at the present time. In part this is related to differences in how long a family has been living in the United States, which varies from more than ten years to less than a month. Of course, the longer the adults have lived in the West, the more exposure to English they have, and the more proficient they become in speaking English. Green and Reder (1986) analyzed the influence of background characteristics on the Hmong adult's acquisition of English. More important than time in the U.S. were three other factors: age, education in Laos, and the ability to read Hmong. It is also commonly found that those adults who are employed by Western businesses, and are thus encouraged to communicate in English by their co-workers, are able to progress in the language more quickly. On the average, the majority of adult Hmong, while not fluent in English, can nevertheless communicate in English to a limited extent. The majority know the alphabet, but find it difficult to read complex sentences and paragraphs. Most can, if forced to, communicate basic needs and ideas.

Hmong elders, which in Hmong society includes some as young as those in their early forties, have a much lower rate of English proficiency. This may be because in this age group, few received more than one to three years of formal education. Also, fewer in this group are encouraged by social service agencies to actively participate in ESL classes and job search activities. Lastly, persons in this age group generally find it more difficult to learn a new language. Moreover, in traditional Hmong culture it is common to find that persons became grandparents as early as when they reached their mid-thirties. Becoming grandparents entitled Hmong persons to go into semi-retirement. They would turn over many responsibilities to their sons and daughters-in-law. Their families would treat them with respect and not ask them to perform any physically or mentally stressful tasks. Thus, it is not uncommon to hear Hmong elders in the United States express the feeling that they are "to old to learn a new language."

Hmong students in California schools today have had experiences very different from their parents, and this will continue to be more and more true as more children are American born. While California schools will seldom need to plan appropriate educational programs for their students' parents, it is important to understand the extent of the parents' exposure to formal education and literacy. The fact that the Hmong come from a remote village lifestyle has as much impact on the success of the children in school as the strength of their various language skills.

The timeline on the following page shows some of the events in the general and educational history of the Hmong that have been mentioned. The shaded figures extend over the portion of that history that has taken place during the lives of Hmong children who reached the ages of 18, 15, 12, and 6, respectively, in 1987. Notice that the oldest of these would only have reached school age at the time when the Hmong began to leave Laos, and that the youngest was probably born in this country and would know of the former life, if at all, only through his or her parents.

Figure 2

Historical Events in the Lifetimes of Hmong Children Now in School

| | 18 yrs old | 15 yrs | 12 yrs | 6 yrs |

1987 Increase in new arrivals to US.
1986 Tertiary migration to Eureka, etc...
1985
1984 ESL/CO, PASS at Phanat Nikhom.
1983 Few Hmong entering US.
1982
1981 Secondary migration to Central Valley.
1980 Peak refugee movement to US. 2,000 Hmong in school at Vinai.
1979 High refugee movement to Thailand and US.
1978 Hmong in camps taught by Vientiane students.
1977
1976 Ban Vinai established. First Hmong settle in California.
1975 Communist takeover of Laos. First refugees escape to Thailand..
1974 "Secret War" ends. Coalition government.
1973 120,000 Hmong in resettlement areas in Laos.
1972
1971 340 Hmong high school students in Vientiane.
1970 37 college students worldwide. Dao Yang is first Hmong to earn Ph.D.
1969
1968 100 village schools, 450 Hmong teachers, 10,000 students
1967 50% of children in resettlement areas attend village schools.
1966 Men serve in the military;
1965 civilians relocated; food
1964 air-dropped; villages burned;
1963 military and civilian casualties.
1962 "Secret War" of Laos begins.
1961
1960
1959 20 Hmong schools, 1500 students. Teachers speak Lao.
1958
1957
1956
1955
1954 Hmong spelling (RPA) standardized. Laos independent of France.

❖ ❖ ❖❖ ❖❖ ❖❖ ❖❖ ❖❖ ❖❖ ❖❖ ❖❖ ❖❖ ❖❖ ❖❖ ❖

Chapter 3

Linguistic Characteristics of the Hmong Language

Relationship of Hmong to Other Languages

It is often stated that Hmong is a member of the broad Sino-Tibetan language family to which the several Chinese languages belong along with Tibetan and some other, lesser-known languages (Greenberg, 1953; Ruhlen, 1976). But the evidence for this claim is not very strong, and some linguists have argued that instead Hmong is a member, along with Thai and Lao, of another great family of languages called Austro-Tai (Benedict, 1985). This family is said to include the Austronesian languages of the Pacific, such as Hawaiian. One linguist has even published evidence purporting to show that Hmong is related to Vietnamese and Cambodian in a third broad family of languages called Austro-Asiatic. Obviously more research is needed before these conflicting claims can be resolved.

What we do know is that Hmong is one of a group of more closely related languages of Southeast Asia and Southern China referred to in the linguistic literature as the Miao-Yao languages. It is the broader, prehistoric affiliations of this sub-family of languages that are in question. The name Miao-Yao is taken from the Chinese names for two groups of people who speak these various related languages, the Miao (including Hmong and others) and the Yao (including some who speak Mien). Only two of these languages are spoken in Laos, namely Hmong and Mien (more precisely *Iu* Mien). So far as we know, all the others are spoken only in Southern China.[3] The Miao people make up the largest of several dozen ethnic minorities in China.

---

[3] There is possibly one other related language in Laos. The name "Black Hmong" is used to refer to two distinct groups of people in Laos. One is a small

The Hmong language is a member of the Miao or "Hmongic" (Strecker, 1981) branch of Miao-Yao. Lemoine (1972) and other scholars recognize three distinct Hmongic languages. These have various names, but following Strecker (1981) we may refer to them by the English names Mhu, Qo Hsiong, and Hmong. Besides being spoken by Hmong people in Laos, Thailand, Burma, and Vietnam, the Hmong language is one of the Hmongic languages most widely spoken in China. Recent studies in China suggest that instead of just three there may be as many as eighteen distinct Hmongic languages, some spoken by small numbers of people (Strecker, 1984).

More distantly, these Hmongic languages are related to the Yao (or Mien) languages which include Iu Mien, spoken in Laos and Thailand as well as China, and five other languages. All of these together make up the Miao-Yao (Hmong-Mien) family.

According to one source (Ruhlen, 1976, p.88) about three million people speak one or another of the Hmong-Mien languages, two-thirds of them in the Chinese province of Kweichow. But this estimate seems conservative. As indicated at the end of Chapter 1, the world Hmong population today seems to be well over five million.

The relationships described here are displayed graphically in Figure 3.

Figure 3   THE HMONG-MIEN FAMILY OF LANGUAGES

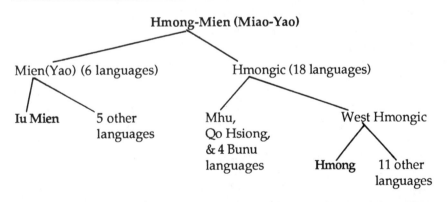

This is a simplified version of a chart given in Ratliff, 1986, p. 30, based on work of David Strecker (unpublished).

group of people who are reported to speak Mhu (see below) rather than Hmong. No speakers of Mhu are known to reside in the United States. The other are actually White Hmong (see below), the name "Black Hmong"" being ascribed to them only by some of their neighbors.

❖Shared Vocabulary Items

One reason why it has been hard to determine family relationships among languages in Asia is that so many vocabulary items and structural properties are shared by various Asian languages regardless of their genetic origins. These similarities seem to be the result of centuries of commerce and cultural interchange among the people of the region. Linguists used to think that Thai was related to Chinese, in the Sino-Tibetan family. Later they decided that it was part of another family of languages, Austro-Tai, but that a lot of words had been taken from Chinese. Now most linguists think that many of the words that are found in both the Thai language and Chinese were originally Austro-Tai, and that the Chinese borrowed them. The same then may apply to the relation between Hmong and Chinese. Although Hmong certainly has some Chinese words as well as Lao words, some of the older words that resemble Chinese words may actually be words that originally were Hmong and that have been taken by the Chinese for their own use. According to Benedict (1985), the Chinese word *Miao* is simply a Chinese form of the word *Hmong*. In any case, many Hmong words have Chinese equivalents, with similar pronunciation. For example, the Hmong and Chinese share many clan names. Thus the Hmong clan name *Vaj* (Vang) corresponds to Chinese *Wang*, Hmong *Lis* (Ly or Li) to Chinese *Lee*, and so on. The Hmong name for French people, *Fab Kis*, comes from a Chinese term for Westerners. Hmong and Chinese have essentially the same word for 'car', spelled *tsheb* in Hmong.

The Hmong have also made up their own new words for some new cultural objects. The standard Hmong word for 'airplane' is *dav hlau*, literally, 'iron hawk'. Similarly, 'train' is *tsheb nqaj hlau*, literally 'vehicle + rail + iron' or 'iron rail vehicle'. A word borrowed from Lao (*lot fai(s)* 'fire vehicle') is also used for 'train.' So Hmong words for modern objects are partly borrowed from Chinese, Lao, Thai, French, and English and partly constructed from native resources.

The following are some words that the *White Hmong-English Dictionary* (Heimbach, 1979) lists as being derived from Chinese and Thai. From Chinese: *cuab* 'a family'; *choj* 'a bridge'; *fab* 'to turn over (as a page, etc.); *feeb* 'fainted, unconscious'; *feem* 'a part, a portion'; *foob xab* 'bellows'; *hwj* (of *fwj*) 'bottle, kettle'; *lim* 'tired, weary'; *maj* 'in a hurry, busy'; *mem* 'ink'. From Thai (or Lao, since in many cases the words are the same or nearly so): *foob* 'to accuse'; *keej* 'clever, quick, intelligent'; *khej* 'crocodile'; *khib* in the expression *khib liab* 'dirty, disgusting'; *khoom* 'goods, baggage'; *loos lees* 'a school' and *loos phav nyas npas* 'hospital'; *lum* 'one dozen'; *moj phob* 'coconut'; *moos* 'the plain, the area down off the mountain; a particular city or market on the plain.' Some words used by Hmong also come from French. Examples are *kav fes* 'coffee' from French *café*, *ka mi oo* 'truck' from French *camion*; *ka noos* 'cannon'; and *kos los nees* 'colonel'.

❖Shared Structural Properties

The Hmong language also shares a number of structural properties with other languages of Asia, such as Chinese. These include, but are not limited to, the following:
1. *a preference for monosyllabic words*
2. *lexical use of tone*
3. *lack of inflections (tense, gender, etc)*
4. *noun classifiers*
5. *serial verb construction.*

Monosyllabic words

Hmong is a predominantly monosyllabic language like Vietnamese and Chinese in contrast to the polysyllabic character of English. Most Hmong words are only one syllable long; those with more than one syllable (seldom more than two) are in nearly all cases made up of syllables that can stand alone as independent words. Thus

---

Implication for Educators:

Help students break polysyllabic English words into syllables that resemble Hmong words. They may be confused by the "schwa" vowel in unaccented syllables; why doesn't an "a" sound like an "a", as in *woman*...why doesn't an "o" sound like an "o", as in *pilot*? Students may assign the syllables tone values, which correspond to the primary and secondary accents on syllables.

Meaning that is carried in written English by punctuation, and orally by sentence intonation, is often carried by use of "particles" that occur at the ends of sentences in oral Hmong. For example, "law" (*lov*) indicates a question that assumes a "yes" answer; "aw" (*os*) softens a command; "nay" (*ne*) implies "you too, what do you say?"; "na" (*naj*) makes the sentence an exclamation.

---

with respect to the size of the words and lack of inflection a Hmong sentence is more like *We all like to see play when we go New York* than like *Everybody enjoys attending theater performances in Chicago.*

Lexical use of tone

Tone is quite different from intonation. In a tonal language like Hmong a particular tone is associated with each syllable and the syllable must be pronounced with this tone. Just as *map* and *mat* and *mad* in English are different words because the final consonants differ, so in Hmong *ma* with high tone or mid tone or low tone is considered three different syllables with three different meanings. Tones in Hmong may differ from one another in relative pitch, in contour (whether rising or falling) and in voice quality (plain or "breathy" or "creaky" voice). Intonation, as in English, uses voice pitch not to distinguish different words but to set questions apart from statements (as in *You did?*) or to express the attitude of the speaker about what he or she is saying.

In Hmong there are eight different tones, two of which may be considered variant realizations of the same tone phoneme. (In contrast, Lao has six and Vietnamese has five to six, depending on the dialect.) These tones are listed in the table below, with the consonant letters used in the Romanized Practical Alphabet (RPA) to spell them.

Figure 4   TONES IN HMONG

Tone	RPA symbol		Example
high tone	-b	*pob*	'ball, lump'
high falling tone	-j	*poj*	'female'
mid rising tone	-v	*pov*	'throw'
mid tone	—	*po*	'spleen'
breathy mid low tone	-g	*pog*	'paternal grandmother'
low tone	-s	*pos*	'thorn'
low falling (creaky) tone	-m	*pom*	'see'

The low rising tone, written -*d*, is found only in the pronunciation in certain contexts (phrase-final) of words that otherwise have the -*m* tone (Heimbach, 1979, Appendix 1, pp. 444-446; see also Ratliff, 1986, pp. 142-145).

Implications for Educators:

Because tone is such an important part of knowing the meanings of words in Hmong, and because English-speaking teachers are not aware that students are attending to the voice pitch of a word, which they interpret as lexical tones, confusions occur. For example, when a speech therapist gives a list of word pairs, and the student is to say "same" or "different" for each pair, a student may pick up the different "tone" of two identical words, and get the item wrong. (Say a word pair like *sat - sat*; notice how your voice indicates *"this is the last word of the pair"* by the falling pitch it gives to the second word; compare it to the pitch of the first word, which means *"another one's coming"*). On the other hand, Hmong students have to learn that in English a word is spelled the same, even if it carries different meaningful tones. For example, a teacher gives the spelling word *bye*. She says this sentence: *John said 'good-bye'.* Then she follows it with, *Bye-bye.* For the Hmong student, the first *bye* in *bye-bye* is different from the second.... two spelling words, not one (in Hmong, *npaiv* and *npais*).

Their awareness of pitch patterns will help students learn the pronunciation of long words. As an example, look at how *America* is spelled in Hmong: *As-mes-liv-kas* or *As-mes-lis-kas.*

The particular voice pitch and intonation of a phrase as it's first learned carries over despite different situations. In English, we judge the sincerity or emotionality of how something's said. For example, *how are you?*—we can tell if the person really wants to know, or is just giving a standard response along with *hello.* However, often the Hmong speaker says *how are you* in exactly the same way, whether he's really interested in knowing or not. Along this same line, sarcasm and irony in English is conveyed with intonation, along with gestures or facial expressions in context. If Hmong speakers are not tuned into these other aspects of conveying meaning, they may miss the sarcastic intent of a comment, and respond literally. Consider the frequent use of *Oh, great,* in various situations (just received a check in the mail, just spilled coffee on my clothes), or the teen-ager's sardonic comment to someone who brags about an accomplishment: *You're my hero.*

Sentence intonation in English is often confusing as well. *Why can't you go?* has the same intonation as a statement, but the listener has to pick up the *why* and the *can't* to understand that it's a question. *Can't* is easy to confuse with *can*, especially for listeners not accustomed to hearing final consonant clusters. Make sure to restate your question, if you don't receive an answer as you expect; it could be that the listener missed the fact that you asked a question.

Lack of Inflections (tense, gender, and so on)

In Hmong, words do not have any inflected forms such as are used in English to indicate the plural and possessive of nouns (*boy, boys, boy's, boys'*), the different genders and cases of pronouns (*he, his, him, she, her, it, its,* etc) or the present, past, gerund, and participle of verbs (*take, takes, took, taking, taken; walk, walks, walked, walking,* etc).

53

Hmong words have only one form. Number, case, tense, etc., are indicated by the order of words and by combinations of words, just as in English the future is represented by *will go* or *going to go,* or the perfect by contrasting *have walked* with the simple past *walked.* Although the Hmong word *kuv* means either 'I' or 'my,' the meaning in any given sentence is clear from the position of the word alone: *kuv noj* is 'I eat,' and *kuv tsev* is 'my house'; before a verb *kuv* means 'I', before a noun it means 'my'. Because of the lack of inflection, Hmong sentences are more like *Two man come past-time enter Joe house* than like English *Two men came to Joe's house.* Obviously, either version would express the meaning equally well.

Implications for Educators:

Teachers assume that a reader will know that the vocabulary word *rode* is the past tense of *ride;* second language learners have to learn that they are the same, except for time; on the other hand, English will use *rice* whether it's *in the field, hulled* or *unhulled,* or *cooked, glutinous* or *plain.* Hmong has different words for rice in different contexts.

When teaching the vocabulary in a reading group, look through the story for items that second language learners may need to learn; look for past tense verbs, contractions, idioms, verbs like *get up, get down, get over,* and culturally different concepts. Prepare to teach each of these with its corresponding other forms. For example, teach *will not* along with *won't;* teach *peanut, peanut butter, jelly,* and *sandwich* along with *peanut butter and jelly sandwich;* teach informal spoken forms like *no way* along with the more formal *impossible;* teach *legislature* along with *Legislature,* pointing out what the capital L signifies; teach *legislate, legislation,* and *legislator* as well, showing how each form is used (noun, verb, adjective, etc). For high school students, one of the most difficult areas of writing is knowing which form of a word to use. Common errors include *I interested in it. I am boring. Did you reservation us a room?* and so on.

A related difficulty is the use of many near-synonyms in English, that correspond to only one word in Hmong. Teach the shades of meaning, using opposite pairs when possible. For example, *txaus-siab* means literally *sufficient-heart/liver* in Hmong; it's used in contexts where an English speaker might choose any of the following near-synonyms: *satisfied, happy, proud, pleased...*

Hmong uses proverbs, sayings, and adages frequently, especially to teach behavior, values, or beliefs. Teachers can make use of this by using proverbs from many cultures to explain classroom events, and the exercise of trying to find a proverb from one's own background that expresses the same message helps language development as well as cross-cultural understanding. As an example, *no man is an island* is similar to a Lao proverb that *one stake cannot make a fence.* In English, *we kill two birds with one stone,* and in Chinese, people *get two eagles with one arrow.* Whenever possible teach concepts by using parables or example stories.

Noun classifiers

Nouns in Hmong are divided into a large number of different classes, similar to genders (masculine, feminine, neuter) but based on categories other than sex. Like gender classes, this classification is partly based on meaning and partly arbitrary. In most uses a noun must be preceded by a word (called a *classifier* by grammarians) that denotes its class membership. Thus *tsev* 'house' takes the classifier *lub* to make *lub tsev* 'the house', but *tub*, meaning 'boy,' takes the classifier *tus* so that 'the boy' is *tus tub*. Sometimes a noun has different meanings depending on which classifier is used; for example, *ntawv* has a general meaning of 'paper.' *Daim ntawv* (with the classifer *daim*, used for flat things) means 'sheet of paper'; *phau ntawv*, with a different classifier, *phau*, means 'book'; *tsab ntawv* means 'letter (written message).' (Heimbach, 1979, p. 187). This feature is shared with other Asian languages including Vietnamese and Chinese.

Implications for Educators:

The use of classifiers defines how things are put together into groups, and there are differences in how a Hmong categorizes things and how English speakers categorize things. For example, in Hmong, a thread, a lifetime, and a road all take the same classifier (*txoj xov, txoj sia, txoj kev*), and therefore share an attribute (length). When psychologists have a bilingual paraprofessional translate the Peabody Picture Vocabulary Test to estimate native language intelligence, there are some major problems. A test page shows four pictures, and the tester says a word, like *farmer*; the child points to the correct picture. If only one of the pictures is a human, then the classifier that goes with the word gives away the answer (*tus neeg ua teb*, or *classifer for humans-person-do-field*).

Another implication is that classification according to English attributes is an important activity for English language development, and involves culture to a great extent. Classification of colors along the spectrum is one example. English speakers have different words for *gray* and *beige*, but in Hmong they are not differentiated. It's not because they can't see the difference, only that they don't have names for all the same parts of the spectrum. Native English speakers begin a public address, "*Ladies and gentlemen...*"; Hmong begin "*clanmates and in-laws*". Hmong groups young children together, and has a different category for young people of marriageable age, and a third for adults. When we regard the marrying of a thirteen-year-old bride as a child marriage, Hmong disagree; it's appropriate because she's *tus hluas nkauj* ('young unmarried girl,' not a 'child,' *tus menyuam*).

Serial verb construction

Another feature that Hmong shares with Chinese languages is the use of so-called "serial verbs" (Owensby, 1986). This term refers to the use of two main verbs in one clause without an 'and' or other connective between them. In English it would be ungrammatical to say something like *I took a book went studied at the library,* but not in Hmong. In Hmong one says the equivalent of *I go arrive his house* where an English speaker would say *I go to his house.* English allows more than one main verb in a clause only in a narrowly restricted set of cases, such as *I'll go buy some milk,* but not *I went bought some.* But Hmong uses this kind of construction very broadly, in cases where the English equivalent would coordinate the verbs with *and* or subordinate one of the verbs, as is the case in *He walked along whistling* or *He whistled as he walked along.*

Implications for Educators:

A written story read aloud sounds different from an story told from memory. Students will need to learn how the written form follows rules that give it a different style than oral language. Native English speaking students learn from kindergarten on the appropriate form for correct written English; a Hmong student has to contend with formulating thoughts in a second language plus the correct form for written English. Often students will write as they speak, and then wonder why it's not acceptable. A good exercise is to let students struggle with writing Hmong, so that when it's read aloud it retains the essential expression of the oral form. The student should record on cassette someone telling a folktale, then transcribe part of it into Hmong. (Take a look at the paper; probably there are no breaks between words, no punctuation, no capitals, no quotations, no beginning or end visible.) Ask the student to read the Hmong aloud, and compare it with the cassette. Ask, "How can you show that these words are what the orphan is saying? How can you show this is a question? Do you need to write down all the sounds? How can you break this up into chunks, into paragraphs, sentences?"

Ask the student to translate the Hmong paragraph into English. Because of the carryover from Hmong, there will be sentences with no subjects, several verbs one after another, liberal use of dialogue, and much replication of structure; the student will have to struggle with the same questions of written style when using English.

❖Distribution of Languages in Laos

The nation of Laos is made up of many distinct peoples, each with their own language. These peoples are referred to in Laos by geographical groupings: the people of the lowlands, the "hill peoples" and the highland people.

The language most widely spoken is Lao, the language of the lowland Lao people, which is the national language. The Lao live in the river valleys, where they grow rice in irrigated plots. The Lao are tied together by their common belief in Buddhism. Their language, closely related to Thai, is written with an alphabetic script based on those used in India, and quite different from the roman alphabet used in the western world.

The foothills between the lowlands and the mountains are inhabited by the Khmu people, who are descendants of the original inhabitants of the country. They grow both wet rice and mountain rice. Their language is completely distinct from Lao, and like the Hmong, they are animists rather than Buddhists.

The Hmong people are the most numerous of the "highland tribes," and, at least until 1975, their language was the most widely spoken of the minority languages. As noted in the first chapter, the Hmong tend to live in small villages at the highest elevations, near the summits of the mountains. Their religion is a form of animism, and their principal crop is dry mountain rice. In recent years, in large part because of the fighting in the mountains, and the devastation of the highland areas caused by American bombs, many Hmong have moved to the mountain valleys or to lowland areas, and some have begun growing irrigated rice.

There are smaller numbers of people belonging to other ethnic groups in the highlands. The Mien (called Yao by others) speak a language that is closely related to Hmong, but not so close that the Hmong and Mien can understand each other. As with the Hmong, some Mien have fled Laos since 1975, going to Thailand and the U.S. as refugees. Another highland people, also represented among refugees in the U.S., are the Thai Dam or "Black Thai." Their language is related to but distinct from Thai and Lao. Several other highland tribes, each with a distinct language, are found in smaller numbers in the mountainous areas of Laos. In addition, traders and artisans from China, Vietnam, and even India visit the towns and villages of northern Laos where the Hmong live. In places where the Hmong have had close contact with members of these other groups, whether because they live in neighboring villages or they come in as itinerant traders, some members of each Hmong village have often learned to communicate in the other languages (Downing, Dunnigan, and Smalley, n.d.; Smalley, 1985). Because Lao is the language of government, business, and education in Laos, most Hmong adults know some Lao and some Hmong speak and read Lao very well.

Dialects of Hmong

The Hmong of Laos recognize two distinct "types" of Hmong people, cutting across clan membership and differing in costume, customs, and dialect. These kinds of Hmong, and the dialects they speak, are called in Hmong *Hmoob Dawb* (in English transliteration 'Hmong Daw'), meaning 'White Hmong' and *Moob Ntsuab* ('Mong Njua'), which is rendered in English as either 'Green Hmong' or 'Blue Hmong.' The colors in these names are based on colors used in the traditional women's costumes of the different groups, an obvious manifestation of their somewhat different cultural heritages. (In Laos some White Hmong are called "Black Hmong," but they are in fact White Hmong and that is what they prefer to be called.) The use of both 'Green' and 'Blue' in English to translate *Moob Ntsuab* results in part from the fact that the word *ntsuab* denotes a segment of the color spectrum that ranges over part of what in English is blue as well as green (Heimbach, 1979). Possibly American speakers choose the term *blue* because the Hmong costumes seen in America are more often blue than green. But *green* seems to better represent the meaning of the Hmong term, so 'Green Hmong' is to be preferred. To add to the complexity of names, members of the Green Hmong group also use and sometimes prefer the name *Moob Leeg* ('Mong Leng'). The spellings *Moob* rather than *Hmoob* and *Mong* rather than *Hmong* reflect the pronunciation of speakers of the Green Hmong dialect, to be discussed below.

❖Mutual Intelligibility

The differences between the dialects, which seem to be no greater than those that differentiate British and American English, do not seem to present serious obstacles to communication, although some (especially White Hmong) claim to have difficulty understanding speakers of the other dialect. The existence of these dialectal differences, and the other cultural differences that distinguish the two groups, is clear evidence that at some time the ancestors of the two groups lived in different places in China, with the separation lasting long enough for the speech of the separate regions to grow different.

Now, after years of living side by side, especially in the crowded conditions of the refugee camps, many Hmong have learned to understand and even to speak both dialects quite readily.

❖Relative Status

Neither dialect has ever had any official status and there are no grounds for preferring one dialect over the other. Nevertheless, White Hmong has been favored in some ways, in that the writing system most commonly used, the Romanized Practical Alphabet (see below), generally comes closer to White Hmong pronunciation, and the most accessible grammars and dictionaries of Hmong produced to date explicitly represent only the White Hmong dialect. Probably also, in Laos, more of those with some education were speakers of White Hmong. Even the English name *Hmong* (rather than *Mong*) represents White Hmong pronunciation. There are, however, also Green Hmong grammars and dictionaries (Lyman, 1974, 1979; Xiong, Xiong and Xiong, 1983), as well as instructional material and stories written in a spelling that represents Green Hmong.

The principal differences between the Green and White Hmong dialects will be described below when we will consider also some problems that the existence of two dialect groups have presented in efforts to establish a uniform writing system.

Implications for Educators:

Both the Green Hmong and the White Hmong dialects are spoken by Hmong people living in California, and both will often be found among students in the same classroom. For this reason the existence of two distinct dialects of Hmong should always be kept in mind when dealing with Hmong students. Explanations or instructions given in Hmong may not be readily understood when the speaker and hearer do not share the same dialect. The same Hmong word in some cases may have slightly or considerably different meanings for speakers of the two dialects. And, unlike English where a standard written form masks dialectal differences, written materials in Hmong may reflect the pronunciation and vocabulary of the speakers of one dialect, making them less accessible or at least less acceptable to speakers of the other dialect.

Differences Between Hmong and English

❖Grammar

In some ways the grammar of Hmong is similar to that of English. A simple sentence in Hmong will usually have subject, verb, and object in that order just as in English. Hmong has prepositions used before noun objects, has helping verbs preceding main verbs, and constructs complex and compound sentences in similar ways.

But there are probably even more ways in which the languages are different. The most important, perhaps, is the complete lack of inflected (affixed) forms of words, which has already been noted.

As also noted above, there are no forms marked for gender in Hmong, so the problem of referring to a person without regard to sex (English *his/her occupation*) does not arise; however, lack of this distinction in Hmong can lead to misuse of *he* and *she* in English. In English whole sets of related words are often derived by adding prefixes and suffixes to a root word, as in *slow, slower, slowly; plant, implant, planter, plantation; govern, government, governor*. Again, Hmong has few sets of related words of this sort, and instead often uses a single form as verb, noun, or adjective, with no change of form, as English also does in some cases: *to play, a play, a play gun*. When big words are made from smaller ones in Hmong, the process is more like that used in English compounds like *car-sick, sick-bed, bedroom, roommate*, etc., where both parts are independent words rather than a root plus an affix.

Besides these differences in word-formation or morphology, there are important word order differences as well. In Hmong, adjectives and other modifiers follow rather than precede the nouns they modify. Thus the Hmong word for 'airplane' is *dav hlau*, literally 'iron hawk', from *dav* 'hawk, large bird' + *hlau* 'iron'. Questions are formed by adding question words, rather than by intonation or by changing the word order.

Two other important features of Hmong grammar that make it different from English have already been described: the pervasive use of classifiers to introduce nouns (English says *one sheet of paper* but not *one person of child*) and the serial verb construction, which allows a single subject to combine with more than one verb to form a single clause (English permits *I'll run get you a paper*, but not *I ran picked brought back some berries*).

These differences between languages may lead to errors when a Hmong student is learning to speak and write English (Dwyer, 1982). For example, a Hmong student wrote *I trip from Bonvinai to Bangkok and is 12 hours go by bus and car*, where *I trip* should be *my trip* and the second verb, *go*, should be changed to *going* or omitted. Dwyer found in her analysis of errors in compositions written by Hmong college students that the most frequent errors involved using the base form of the verb instead of the appropriate inflected present or past tense forms. For example a student wrote *After breakfast I bring lunch and I am carrying my bag then I go in the bus*. The next most frequent type of error was in the use of pronouns. When the number of incorrect uses of a given construction was compared with the number of correct uses of the same construction, other errors showed up as the most frequent. The constructions that students got wrong more than 50% of the time were as follows:

there is; there are (omitted)	71%
present perfect	62%
be + verb + *ing*	61%
passive	60%
present tense (uninflected)	52%

Note that these are all errors in the use of verb forms. Other errors included omission of articles; use of a pronoun to duplicate a noun subject (e.g., *John he left*); omission of plural marker on nouns; omission of subject pronoun *I* or *we*; and misuse or omission of prepositions (Dwyer, 1982, p. 235). Dwyer also found (p. 236) that "Hmong learners share many of the most frequent errors with learners of many other native language backgrounds."

❖Vocabulary

One difference with regard to vocabulary mentioned above is the formation of new words by compounding rather than by the use of affixes like *re-*, *un-*, *-ly*, and *-ation*, which is so common in English but doesn't exist in Hmong.

Another striking difference is that Hmong simply doesn't have any commonly accepted term for many of the objects and concepts that are familiar to people living in the American culture. Of course, speakers of English similarly would have no words to name many things such as plants, animals, foods, spirits, and practices that are familiar parts of life in Laos. When a language lacks words for some new object, concept, or institution, the gaps are usually filled by deriving new words from old ones or, more commonly, by importing them from languages where the needed words already exist. The English language has "borrowed" terms from other languages for many feature of Western educational practices, for example, over the past several hundred years. The English words *school, kindergarten, elementary, education, course, gymnasium, library, mathematics, civics, schedule, instruction, college, university,* and most other school terms have been brought into English in this way, from Greek, Latin, French and other languages. In Laos, formal education was conducted in the Lao and French languages, so those who went to school used Lao and French terms to talk about education, and few of these words have made their way into the Hmong vocabulary. Consequently, it is sometimes difficult even to translate information about educational and other activities into Hmong in a way that will be generally understood without explanation. Among the American school concepts for which Hmong provides no clear equivalent are such expressions as *course of studies, recess, register, promotion, citizenship grade, schedule, graduation requirements, and physical education (PE).*

Implications for Educators:

When translating or interpreting for Hmong parents about school-related concepts, it's necessary to explain the "American" views on which the concepts are based. Often there is no equivalent concept in Hmong, so that translation/interpretation alone does not mean that communication and understanding take place. For example, the American concepts of "potential", "intelligence", "learning handicapped", "gifted", "under-achiever" and so on all depend on a general concept of something unseen within a person that can be measured, and then increased or decreased. The Hmong don't have distinctions in the language to differentiate between a child's *potential* to perform vs. his actual *performance.* What a person *does* is what he *can* do; therefore, a student who gets C's and D's cannot be in the same category as a student who gets A's and B's. Parents will need to understand how a student with C's may be in a program for the gifted, but a student with A's is not. Likewise, they will need to understand that there are ways to change or enhance the performance of children with blindness, deafness, physical disability, retardation, or learning handicaps. Before involving parents in home strategies to teach a deaf child to function in a hearing world, the parents need to understand that Americans truly believe that it's possible to change that child; Hmong probably believe that it's their turn to have a deaf child born to them, and that that child will be taken care of throughout his/her life (he/she will no doubt marry a hearing person); the way in which the family cares for the child will influence their descendants' lives.

The best way for the translator/interpreter to learn these basic American concepts is to work day to day in an environment where he/she can see "with his own eyes" different situations and their outcomes.

The native Hmong vocabulary includes only a small number of unanalyzable two-syllable words. Often one part has an independent meaning and the other part does not, but there is never an reason to call the latter an affix. Here are some examples of these few unanalyzable native two-syllable words.

tagkis	'tomorrow'	from *tas* 'finish' + *kis* (no meaning)
nimno	'now'	from *nim* (no meaning) + *no* 'this'
twjywm	'be quiet'	neither syllable has an independent meaning

Usually, two-syllable words are compounds, made up of clearly recognizable components. These are of at least two types. The first type is similar to English compounds like *lamp post, coffee cake,* or *blackboard* except that in Hmong the modifier follows its head. Here are some examples:

hwj kais	'teapot'	*hwj* 'kettle'	*kais* 'spout'
paj kws	'popcorn'	*paj* 'flower'	*kws* 'corn'
paj ntaub	'embroidery'	*paj* 'flower'	*ntaub* 'cloth'
paj lug	'flowery speech'	*paj* 'flower'	*lus* 'word'
roj npua	'pig fat'	*roj* 'oil, fat'	*npua* 'pig'
roj av	'kerosene'	*roj* 'oil, fat'	*av* 'earth, ground'
chaw pw	'sleeping place, bed, bedroom'	*chaw* 'place, region'	*pw* 'to lie down; to sleep'
chaw noj mov	'eating room, kitchen'	*chaw* 'place, region'	*noj mov* 'to eat rice'
niam hlau	'magnet'	*niam* 'wife'	*hlau* 'iron'

A second type of compound involves the juxtaposition of two nouns (or other elements) to form an expression with a meaning broader than that of either component. Neither element is a "head".

niam txiv	'parents'	*niam* 'mother'	*txiv* 'male, father'
kwv tij	'brother, brethren'	*kwv* 'younger brother'	*tij* 'older brother'
me nyuam	'small; child, children'	*me* 'small'	*nyuam* 'little, negligible'

This second type of compounding is not common in English, but the first of course is. All types of word-building through affixation or stem changes (*swim, swam, swum,* etc) will be unfamiliar to the Hmong student from his/her experience with the Hmong language.

❖Pronunciation and Spelling

The RPA

The Romanized Practical Alphabet (RPA), devised for Hmong in the 1950's by missionary linguists and employed by most literate Hmong in the United States, uses only the ordinary letters of the roman alphabet with no diacritic symbols. In this respect it is just like English. Children learning to read both Hmong and English thus have only one set of letters to learn. However, the letters do not all represent similar sounds in the two languages, which could cause some difficulty for learners. The RPA is a phonemic writing system, meaning that there is one unique and consistent way of writing each distinctive sound, including consonants, vowels, and tones. We can thus use this writing system to discuss the sound pattern or pronunciation of Hmong, and thus avoid the need for phonetic symbols. In this section we will introduce the Romanized Practical Alphabet and the sounds of Hmong that the RPA letters represent and show the major points of difference between Hmong and English.

Syllables

A syllable in Hmong has three distinct parts: consonant, vowel, and tone. The consonant is optional, but there must be a vowel, and it must be pronounced on one or the other of the tone levels. A consonant or consonant cluster, when present, begins the syllable, which then ends with a vowel or diphthong. There is never a consonant sound at the end of the word, with one exception. Some words, like *Hmong*, may end with a velar nasal (the *-ng* sound). But for many Hmong, such words have only a nasalized vowel, rather than a vowel followed by a nasal consonant. For these people, Hmong syllables never have final consonants. The tone is heard on the vowel itself, but in the RPA the choice of tone is indicated by a consonant letter written after the vowel. The word *tsheb* 'vehicle', for example, consists of the consonant spelled *tsh* plus the vowel *e* pronounced on the high tone indicated by the final *-b*.

Consonants

One of the distinctive characteristics of the Hmong languages is the large number of different consonant sounds with which words may begin. In the RPA a single consonant sound may be represented by a sequence of one to four letters, each letter indicating one feature of the sound. In the example above, the *t* shows that the consonant begins with a stop, the *s* indicates fricative release, and the *h* shows that the release is aspirated (breathy).

Table 5 (based on Ratliff 1986, p. 16, modified form Jarkey 1986) shows all of the Hmong consonants with their RPA spellings. In the table the columns, headed by capital letters, denote differences in manner of release (plain, lateral, r-like [rhotic] or fricative) and place of articulation, from the lips (A) to the glottis (M) as follows:

A	bilabial
B	bilabial with lateral release
C	labio-dental
D	apico-dental
E	apico-dental affricate (i.e., fricative release)
F	lamino-dental with palatal offglide
G	apico-alveolar
H	lamino-alveolar
I	apico-post-alveolar with rhotic release
J	palatal
K	velar
L	uvular
M	glottal

The rows represent differences in the manner of articulation. There are four series of stopped consonants (1-4), voiced and voiceless fricatives (5-6), and nasals, liquids, and a single voiced glide (7-10).

A more detailed version of the same chart, including a precise phonetic representation of each sound as pronounced in the White Hmong dialect is given in Table 1 of Appendix D.

There are four series of stopped consonants (stops and affricates) in Hmong. The first has no aspiration, like the stops *p, t,* and *k* in French or Spanish. The second series has aspiration, like the more breathy initial *p, t, k* in English. Aspiration is represented in the RPA spelling by the letter *h* following the stopped consonant. The third series adds pre-nasalization without aspiration, spelled with initial *n*, as in the word *nkauj* 'song' or *ntoos* 'tree.' The fourth series has both pre-nasalization and aspiration. Each series includes nine or ten different stops or affricates (stops with a fricative release), pronounced in different positions and in different manners, from the front to the back of the mouth, making 38 different stopped consonants in all.

The next two series are the fricative consonants. These are either voiced (*v* and *z*), or unvoiced, like *f, x* (representing the 's' sound), *s* (representing the 'sh' sound), *xy,* and *h*.

Table 5 RPA CONSONANT SPELLINGS

	A	B	C	D	E	F	G	H	I	J	K	L	M
STOPS & AFFRICATES													
1	p	pl		t	tx	c	d	ts	r		k	q	
2	ph	plh		th	txh	ch	dh	tsh	rh		kh	qh	
3	np	npl		nt	ntx	rc		nts	nr		nk	nq	
4	nph	nplh		nth	ntxh	nch		ntsh	nrh		nkh	nqh	
FRICATIVES													
5			v					z					
6			f		x			s		xy			h
NASALS, LIQUIDS, & GLIDES													
7	m	ml		n						ny	g		
8	hm	hml		hn						hny			
9				l									
10				hl									
11										y			

(based on Ratliff 1986, p. 16, modified from Jarkey 1986)

A bilabial
B bilabial with lateral release
C labio-dental
D apico-dental
E apico-dental affricate (i.e., fricative release)
F lamino-dental with palatal offglide
G apico-alveolar
H lamino-alveolar
I apico-post-alveolar with rhotic release
J palatal
K velar
L uvular
M glottal

The remaining sounds are the nasals (rows 7 and 8), the liquids (rows 9 and 10) and the single glide sound *y* (row 11). Both nasal and liquid (l-like) consonants occur in two series in the White Hmong dialect: those with a plain voiced sound, as in English *no* and *look*, and those that are pronounced without voicing, giving a whispered quality. In these series, voicelessness is indicated by writing *h* before the voiceless sound. An example would be the name *Hmong*, with a voiceless *m* in contrast with the voiced *m* of the Hmong word *mob* 'hurt.' The Green Hmong dialect does not have the second series, so speakers of that dialect may write the name of their language as *Mong* in English, *Moob* in RPA spelling. The Hmong letter *g* at the beginning of a word represents the sound spelled *ng* in English, found in only a few Hmong words.

Even though Hmong has many more consonants than English, there are still a few English sounds that are not found in Hmong and that may therefore be difficult for the learner. These include the two *th*-sounds (the sounds of *thistle* and *this*), the sounds *z* and *w*, and the voiced stops *b* and *g*, and the affricate spelled *j* or *dg* in English, as in *judge*. White Hmong has a *d*, but in Green Hmong the letter *d* is pronounced *tl* (often spelled *dl*). Hmong has no sound like English *r*; the letter *r* is used in Hmong for a kind of *t*-sound. Table 3 of Appendix D shows all of the distinctive sounds of English; those sounds with no close equivalent in Hmong are enclosed in boxes.

Vowels

Hmong has six simple vowels, written *a, e, i, o, u,* and *w*. The *w* is pronounced like the vowel in the second syllable of English *roses*. There are also two nasalized vowels (three in Green Hmong), which as already mentioned may be followed by a velar nasal (*-ng*). Nasalization is represented in the RPA orthography only by doubling the vowel letter: *ee, oo,* and *aa*. Hmong also has five diphthongs, including *ai* and *au*, which are like the vowels of English *high* and *how*, and *ia, ua,* and *aw*, which have no English counterparts, but are essentially sequences of the simple vowels, pronounced with a single tone. The three classes of Hmong vowels are shown in Table 6 below, arranged according to their place of articulation. Table 2 in Appendix D shows the same vowel spellings but includes a phonetic representation of each sound as pronounced in the White Hmong dialect.

The differences between Hmong and English vowels seem to present few problems for learners, even though English has several vowels that are not found in Hmong. Table 3 in Appendix D shows the English vowels, with those that are most different from Hmong vowels presented in boxes.

Table 6 HMONG VOWELS

	ORAL				NASAL		
FRONT	CENTRAL	BACK			FRONT	CENTRAL	BACK
i	w	u		HIGH			
e		o		MID	ee		oo
	a			LOW		aa	

	DIPHTHONGS						
i a	ua	aw	a i	au			

Tones

The most striking feature of the RPA is the use of consonant letters written at the ends of syllables to represent the different tones on which the vowel may be pronounced.

The eight tones of Hmong, each represented in spelling by a different consonant letter written after the vowel, were introduced earlier. Briefly, the eight tones are as follows: high (spelled -*b*), high falling (-*j*), mid rising (-*v*), mid (--), breathy mid-low (-*g*), low (-*s*), low falling (-*m*), and low falling and rising (-*d*). The *m*-tone is sometimes produced with a creaky voice quality and may even be cut short by glottal closure. The *d*-tone is a predictable variant of the *m*-tone, occurring in certain syntactic positions within the sentence.

Tone shifts

Besides the regular alternation between the *m* and *d* tones, there are some predictable shifts that take place between other tones. For example, when a syllable that ordinarily has the -*s* tone follows a high (-*b* or -*j*) tone, it is pronounced with the "breathy" tone (-*g*). This shift is usually represented in spelling, so the same word might be written *tus* or *tug*, for example, depending on which tone is used in the particular context.

The difficulty of English final consonants

Even after a Hmong student learns to pronounce all of the sounds of English, he or she may still have problems with certain positions and sequences in which the sounds occur. English has long words with two or more syllables, some stressed and others unstressed, and the vowels may sound different in unstressed syllables. English also has sequences or clusters of consonants that are not found in Hmong as in *strengthen* and *squash* and *twelfths*. These will need special attention.

The most difficult aspect of pronunciation for Hmong speakers learning English has to do with the consonants that come at the ends of words, following the vowel. Unlike Hmong, English has both single consonants and consonant clusters in this position, as in the words *farmed* (pronounced [-rmd]), *warmth, mixed* [-kst], *curbed* [-rbd], etc. These final clusters are especially important in English because they include derivational suffixes, such as *-th*, and grammatical suffixes such as the plural and possessive of nouns, and the past tense of verbs.

Implications for Educators:

Hmong students often fail to pronounce all the consonants at the end of an English word because (1) their language doesn't allow consonants after vowels and especially the sequences of consonants founds in English; (2) Hmong uses separate words to express the tense of verbs and the number (singular/plural) of nouns; and (3) Hmong words don't permit modification by suffixes—each Hmong words has just one form. To a Hmong student the "endings" that English speakers consider so natural and so important seem unimportant, unnecessary, and difficult to pronounce. Without special encouragement students may therefore omit them, not only in speaking but in writing.

A resource that can be used to help Hmong students with English pronunciation is *English Pronunciation Lessons for Hmongs* (National Indochinese Clearinghouse, 1980).

Figure 5 SAMPLE TEXT: (GREEN) HMONG IN RPA SPELLING

This example is a proverb in Green Hmong from *Grandmother's Path,
Grandfather's Way* (Vang and Lewis, 1984, p. 78):

*Tau yaam tshab txhob hnov qaab yaam qub
Tau nam yau ncu ntsoov nam hlub.*

[get-thing-new-don't-forget-thing-old
get-wife-young-remember-well-wife-older]

*Accept the new things, but don't forget the old things;
Take a new wife, but don't forget the first wife.*

Figure 6 SAMPLE TEXT: (WHITE) HMONG IN RPA SPELLING

The example that follows is a simple story taken from a beginning Hmong
reader, *Kawm Ntawv Hmoob, Phau 1*, published in Thailand. The
repetitiveness is not characteristic of of the Hmong language in general but of
the literacy materials from which it is drawn.

mus plob
'Going Hunting'

tuam xav mus plob	'Tua wanted to go hunting.'
tsav kuj xav mus plob thiab	'And Cha wanted to go hunting too.'
tuam txawm kwv phom	'And so Tua carried a gun (on his shoulder).'
tsav kuj kwv phom thiab	'And Cha also carried a gun (on his shoulder).'
tuam thiab tsav mus plob lawm	'Tua and Cha have gone hunting.'
nkawd tsis tau los tsev li	'The two of them have not yet come home.'

Vocabulary:

kuj	and	plob	to hunt
kwv	to carry on the shoulder	tau	to be completed
lawm	already	thiab	also, and
li	final particle	tsav	Cha (boy's name)
los	to return	tsev	house
mus	to go	tsis	not
nkawd	the two, both	tuam	Tua (boy's name)
phom	gun	txawm	thus, so
		xav	to want

Other Hmong Writing Systems

One often hears it said that Hmong was until recently an unwritten language, that it has been a written language for only about thirty years.

There is a sense in which this is true, but it is also misleading in certain respects. First of all the implication that there are two distinct types of language involved must be challenged. All languages that are learned by children from their elders are primarily systems for oral use; a means of writing down words and sentences of the language may or may not exist, and a very small or a very large percentage of those who speak the language may also be literate, that is, able to write it and to read what is written. The basic nature of the language is unaffected by these uses of the language; languages that are written are neither more complex, nor more complete, nor more logical, etc., than those that are not.

Secondly, in the case of the Hmong language, various ways of writing it down have existed at various times in its history, and some portion of the population has known and used these systems. Some fascinating aspects of the history of written Hmong are recorded in an article "Les écritures du Hmong" by Jacques Lemoine (1972). In China, Hmong has sometimes been written with Chinese characters, and an idiosyncratic alphabet for Hmong known as the Pollard script was introduced by a missionary in China around 1905.[4]

An anthropologist, Inez de Beauclair, writing in the 1950's of her experiences with the Hmong people in China, wrote that "even the hard-working women of the Great Flowery Miao (i.e., Hmong) know how to read the Pollard script."[5]

Traditional stories of the migration of the Hmong from China to Southeast Asia explain the subsequent illiteracy of the Hmong by saying that these earlier refugees, fleeing from persecution at the hands of the Chinese, and burdened with all their earthly goods, had to choose

---

[4] Pollard, 1919, pp. 173-176. One of the authors has seen a book in this script, published in China, on display in a history of writing exhibit in the British Museum in London.

[5] de Beauclair, "A Miao Tribe of Southeast Kweichow and its Cultural Configuration," in de Beauclair, 1970, p.113.

between leaving their books or their guns behind, and chose to drop the books and keep their only means of protection. Whatever the truth of that story, the Hmong in Laos had no means of writing their language until the middle of this century.

In Thailand and Laos various attempts have been made to adapt the scripts used to write the national languages, based on the Sanskrit and Pali alphabets, to write Hmong and other hilltribe languages. But the most satisfactory and most widely adopted system is the Romanized Practical Alphabet (RPA), described above. This was developed in the early 1950's after careful analysis of the Hmong system of pronunciation in the two major Hmong dialects of Thailand and Laos by the American Protestant missionary linguists J. Linwood Barney and William Smalley. It was later standardized in consultation with French Catholic missionaries who were also introducing literacy to the Hmong in Laos and Thailand at the time.[6] This is the system most often used by Hmong in the United States.

There is another system for writing Hmong which is used by some Hmong in refugee camps in Thailand and by a small but growing number

Figure 7 SAMPLE TEXT: PAHAWH HMONG

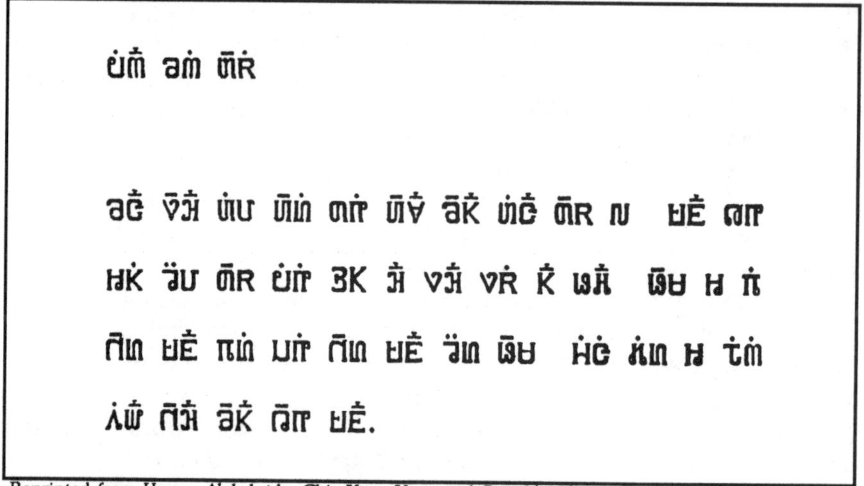

of Hmong in the United States (Bessac, 1982). This system, sometimes referred to as "Chao Fa" writing, originated with a Hmong religious leader, Yang Shong Lue (*Yaj Soob Lwj*) in 1959. It is properly referred to

---

[6] G. Linwood Barney and William A. Smalley, 1953.

as "Pahawh Hmong" (*Phaj hauj Hmoob*) (Smalley, 1987). The characters used are unique, and the system, which exists in at least four different versions is only partly alphabetic. Pahawh Hmong, used principally by religious followers of Yang Shong Lue, is the only completely indigenous writing system for Hmong. Figure 7 shows a sample text written in Pahawh Hmong.

Differences between White and Green Hmong dialects

A person who speaks the Green Hmong dialect can generally understand someone speaking White Hmong without much difficulty, and vice versa. The differences are about as great as those between major regional differences of American and British English. Some words are used in one dialect that are not used in the other, or the same words are used in somewhat different meanings. Pronunciations of words may differ also, and since there is no single accepted, standard way of spelling Hmong, people generally spell words as they pronounce them. Several of these pronunciation differences are systematic, that is, all the words with a certain pronunciation in one dialect will have the same different pronunciation in the other. The most important regular correspondences are these (examples from National Indochinese Clearinghouse, 1978; William Smalley, 1982; and Thao and Robson, 1982).

Figure 8 CORRESPONDENCE BETWEEN WHITE AND GREEN HMONG

Green Hmong		White Hmong		Meaning
Regular correspondence:				
m	Moob	h m	Hmoob	'Hmong'
n	nab	h n	hnab	'bag'
ny	nyav	hny	hnyav	'heavy'

Many words follow this pattern; other words, such as *mem* 'ink' and *nyob* 'be at', are pronounced the same way (without *h-*) in both dialects.

t l	tlej*	d	dej	'water'
t l h	tlha*	d h	dhia	'jump'
ntl	ntlaas*	nt	ntas	'ripple, wave'
ntlh	ntlhi*	nth	nthi	intensifier

---

* also spelled as *dlej, dlha, ndlaas, ndlhi.*

Fairly regular correspondence:

a a	*p a a b*		*a*	*p a b*	'help'
a	*t a b*		*i a*	*t i a b*	'skirt'

Irregular correspondence: (examples are comparable to different pronunciations of English *aunt, roof, route,* or *while* vs. *whilst*):

h a s	*h a i s*	'to speak'
p u j	*p o j*	'female'
k u a s	*k o m*	'to cause'
f e m	*f i m*	'to meet'
m o o g	*m u s*	'to go'
f w j	*h w j*	'bottle'

The RPA orthography was intended for use by speakers of both dialects, with spellings which, although chosen for linguistic and practical reasons, were generally closer to White Hmong pronunciation. But, as noted above, the tendency has been for people to spell words according to pronunciation in their own dialect. In 1982 General Vang Pao organized the Hmong Language Council, consisting of twelve persons representing both dialect groups. At a national conference convened at the University of Minnesota (Thao & Robson, 1982) the Council made an effort to arrive at a compromise spelling. The Council agreed on spellings for the regular correspondence listed above. For example, they proposed to write *Mhoob* instead of *Moob* or *Hmoob* for 'Hmong,' and to spell the word as *Mhong* in English. But there was insufficient time to work out other changes, and those agreed upon have not been generally implemented, since the Council has had no good means of promoting the reforms. One other point of agreement at that meeting was that, insofar as possible, English punctuation conventions should be followed in writing Hmong.

Cultural Patterns and Hmong Language

We have already noted that, in its vocabulary at least, the Hmong language reflects the culture of the people who speak it. It is also true that the spoken word is an integral part of that culture. A

74

major aspect of this interrelationship will be briefly exemplified, relating to forms of address and naming practices within Hmong culture.

❖Forms of Address

Terms used to address others are drawn from kinship terms, indicating perhaps the recency of association with non-kin. Hmong society is divided into two kinds of people: clanmates (*kwv tij*) and in-laws (*neej tsa*). *Kwv tij* are all those who have the same clan affiliation (last name); thus two men of the *Lis* clan unrelated by blood would call each other 'young brother' (*tus kwv*) or 'old brother' (*tij laug*). *Neej tsa* are all other Hmong, or members of clans to whom marriage is allowed. There a different set of kinship terms that are used for *neej tsa*.

Males and females who have the same clan name are brothers and sisters; because of this, no man and woman with the same clan name are allowed to marry, even if they are born and raised in different countries. When two potentially marriageable people meet, the first question to be asked is *Koj yog xeem Hmoob dab tsi?* ('What Hmong clan are you?'). Only if they are of different clans does the conversation continue. Even among younger children, socializing with clanmates of the opposite sex is discouraged.

Other than clan membership, it is the generation level that determines one's relationship to another, and so which form of address to use. All those males of one's same generation are brothers (same clan) or cousins (different clan). Males of the father's generation are "old fathers" or "young fathers" (*txiv hlob, txiv ntxawm*), or in English kinship terms, "uncles". The same pattern holds true for one's grandfather's generation (*yawg* 'grandfather'), or son's generation (*tub*, 'son'). Thus it is important for two men who meet to ask questions to determine whether or not they are of the same clan, and how they relate to one another by generation. Women use kinship terms by generation in much the same way as the men, with different terms for clanmates and non-clanmates.

A married woman retains her own clan name and ties, but refers to people from her husband's point of view, rather than her father's. Thus, the man and woman who raised her are her *neej tsa* 'in-laws', and so on. A married woman is seldom addressed by personal name, but rather by a word that expresses her relationship to her husband, and the husband's relationship to the speaker. Thus, a woman who was *Mim* of the *Hawj* clan as a child, marries *Leej* of the *Vaj* clan and has a son, *Foom*; she is now *niam Leej* 'Leng's wife' or *Foom niam* 'Fong's mother'. Her husband may call her *Mim*, or more frequently, *Foom niam* or *tub niam* 'son's mother'; her husband's mother will call her *nyab* 'son's wife', and so on.

If a person has an official function, then he or she is referred to by that function, like *nom tswv* 'chief', or *xib fwb* 'master' or 'teacher'.

To sum up then, people are either one's clanmates or one's in-laws; of one's own generation, parent's generation, grandparent's generation, or child's generation; there is a specific form of address for each relationship; and use of these terms does not necessarily indicate a close family (bloodline or marriage) relationship as it does in English.

❖Evolution of Hmong Names

Up until the 1940's and in many family groups until the mid-70's, Hmong individuals in Laos bore no surnames. Traditional naming practices, stated briefly are these (Downing and Fuller, 1985).

The naming of newborns, usually done outside the home on the third day after delivery in a ritual ceremony organized by the father, typically involves free choice among the full range of Hmong one-syllable given names. The names *Tub*, meaning 'son' or 'boy' and *Maiv*, 'little girl' are sometimes used as names an sometimes prefixed to the given name, either informally or as a formal part of the name. The word *Ntxhais*, 'girl', 'daughter,' is also used as a girl's name. Otherwise, most names can be used for either a boy or a girl, although some names are customarily considered boys' or girls' names. Gender ambiguity can be eliminated by use of the appropriate prefixed name.

Occasionally a child may be given more than one name. One example is when the child is named for a famous person, such as Kong Meng (*Koob Meej*), or Vang Pao (*Vaj Pov*).

Another instance where a child may have two names is when boys are named according to their birth order, in a pattern apparently adopted from the Chinese; the ordinal numbers used are Chinese words.

Los Tuam	first son (literally 'come first')
Los Lwm	second son
Los Xab	third son
Los Xwm	fourth son
Los Vws	fifth son
Los Lwj	sixth son
Los Txhij	seventh son
Los Puaj	eighth son
Los Caw	ninth son
Los Sij	tenth son

76

Although most Hmong do not actually use these as their sons' given names, they may call them *Los Tuam*, etc., when expressing good wishes toward them or to identify the numerical order of the birth of boys in the family.

While a person normally keeps the same name from birth to death, special circumstances call for changing a child's name. The child may be sick, necessitating change because that name does not have enough power to resist the influences that cause the sickness.

A second type of name change involves the addition of an honorific name given to a man by his wife's family after the birth of one or two children. The additional name, bestowed by the father-in-law but often chosen by the wife or by the individual and his family, is given both to celebrate the fact that the couple is able to have children and to promote good relations between the husband's and wife's clans. Usually the honorific name forms a prefix to the birth name, for example a person named *Pov* might become *Yeeb Pov* or *Tooj Pov*.

Traditionally, there was no surname. Individuals were simply identified as belonging to a certain clan. There are more than twenty Hmong clans and every Hmong individual belongs to a clan—that of one's father or, for a married woman, one's husband. Clans are extremely important in the social structure of the Hmong. Persons of the same clan take responsibility for one another's welfare, so that it is always possible to go to any person who belongs to the same clan for help with a problem or for shelter when traveling. In addition, marriage to another person who belongs to the same clan is prohibited. So it is very important to know to what clan an individual belongs, and thus when strangers meet it is customary to ask each others' clan.

Since the clan is so large and therefore numbers so many members, sub-lineage groups within a clan are also important. Members of the same sub-lineage, usually identified as the descendents of some known ancestor, have special obligations to one another (see Dunnigan, 1982). Therefore when strangers have learned that they belong to the same clan, they will proceed to find out whether they share a lineage. This was done traditionally by inquiry into specific customs, such as burial practices, of the group. Different sub-lineages will have small but significant differences in these practices. Or the individuals will try to find out whether they are descendents of a common male ancestor (e.g., great-grandfather).

To summarize, in traditional Hmong society, individuals were identified by their given names, perhaps augmented by prefixes, and by the name of their clan and the name or practices associated with their sub-lineage. But the clan and lineage names were not used as surnames.

During the 1940's, however, it became the fashion in Laos to adopt Western-style names, which were often required by government authorities. The Hmong, living in remote mountain areas, gradually adopted surnames (or had them assigned by the authorities) as they came into contact with schools, tax collectors, and military paymasters. For the Hmong, since each person was customarily identified by his or her clan membership, clan names quite obviously and automatically became surnames. A person named Leng, belonging to the Vang clan, became Leng Vang; a Moua of the Lee clan became Lee Moua, etc. Children belonged to their father's clan; married women's names were not changed upon marriage, since although they become members of the husband's clan (by adoption) upon marriage, it is still important socially for them to be identified according to their birth clan. Thus Lee Mai might be the wife of Vang Tou.

The order *surname+given name* followed the pattern of Chinese names, and was acceptable to French authorities. But gradually most Hmong have changed to the order *given name+surname which* is used by Lao and Thai as well as Westerners. A few prominent Hmong, however, did not choose clan names as surnames. While Lieutenant (later General) Vang Pao did, Tou By, a government official and son of the great chief Ly Foung, became known as *Touby Lyfoung*—he took the name of a famous member of his sub-lineage as his surname.

There is some evidence from recent name changes that the popularity of clan names as surnames is decreasing. The most common alternative is to use the name of a prominent ancestor, as in the example already given, of *Touby Lyfoung*, whose surname is his father's name *(Foung)* combined with his clan name *(Ly)*. Other such surnames are *Bliatout, Saykao, Vangyi,* and *Lysongtseng.*

Other changes in naming patterns are ongoing as well. For example, young women who have attended high school in this country now often take their husband's name upon marriage to replace their own clan name. This seems to involve the adoption of what they see as the predominant American pattern. And educated Hmong women of all ages, especially those employed professionally, often now use three names: *given name + maiden name* (birth clan) + *husband's clan name,* e.g., *Mo Ly Yang* for a woman whose name before marriage was *Mo Ly.* This, of course, conforms to another American pattern.

Chapter 4

Recommended Instructional and Curricular Strategies
for Hmong Language Development

Hmong refugees in the United States are undergoing rapid changes in their lifestyles, social and economic development, and educational status. From a people who formerly had very low literacy rates, within a decade a new generation of literate children has arisen. However, the majority of effort has been towards obtaining the English speaking and literacy skills necessary to survive in this society. Amongst the children and teen-aged Hmong students, there is evidence that Hmong literacy is not being systematically developed. Efforts to encourage Hmong language development, both communicative and literacy skills, should be taken by both the Hmong communities and the American school systems to ensure that not only do limited English speaking students receive equality of educational opportunity, but that they do not suffer from the effects of subtractive bilingualism (interruption in the acquisition and development of the first language and insufficient acquisition of the second language).

For Hmong adult and teen-aged students, those who are literate in Hmong will probably be easily able to transfer these reading and writing skills to English. This is of course because the majority of Hmong in the United States use the roman alphabet. It is a simple matter for them to adjust to which letters are to be associated with which sounds, and thus to be able to read and write in English.

Those who are literate in their own language have proven that they have the requisite visual, auditory, and sensorimotor skills, as well as oral language conceptual development necessary to learn any language. This means the student has at least minimum skills and abilities, and thus should be able to progress educationally even when taught in a second language.

Another positive effect of native language literacy is that it encourages a sense of pride in the student for having the ability to read and write in his or her own language. It also implies that the student has a positive sense of his or her own identity, is well adjusted to his/her ethnic group, and reflects acceptance and knowledge of his/her culture.

Native language literacy ensures an educated group of fully bilingual-bicultural persons who can be leaders in the fields of education, politics, economics, medicine, and so on. They will doubtless be leaders of their ethnic groups as well as needed liaisons between their communities and the greater society.

Prior to 1975, there was virtually no information on Hmong literacy development. During the past decade, with growing numbers of Hmong refugees resettling in the United States, opportunities for research in this field have opened up. There is still relatively little data available, but several investigators have published papers on this subject. A good example of this is the Language and Literacy section of *The Hmong in Transition,* (Hendricks, Downing & Deinard, editors, 1982) and the report, *Acquisition and Use of Literacy in the Hmong Community of Newton* (Reder, Green, & Sweeney, 1983).

❖Exposure to Language

Students should be exposed to both Hmong and English so that they can become proficient in both languages. School personnel and practices should create an emotional climate that allows students to maintain and develop their primary language skills.

By the age of five or six, all children, except those who are severely retarded, deaf or aphasic, acquire basic interpersonal communicative skills in Hmong, spoken in the home and community. However, unless taught in a planned program, students will not proceed to cognitive or academic language proficiency in Hmong (cognitive or academic language skills are those associated with literacy and school achievement). The home, the school, and the community are all appropriate settings for such development of primary language skills.

Parents and older siblings can be encouraged and taught to work with preschool and school aged children in a variety of activities. Teachers in American classrooms often tell language minority parents to speak English more at home. Unfortunately, such a practice is often not possible or even desirable. Speaking torturous or broken English may severely limit the quantity and quality of verbal interaction between parents and children. Rather, teachers can encourage parents to verbalize with children in their strongest language in ways that build underlying cognitive skills. For example, many parents, especially those who have never been to school, are not familiar with the ritual

80

that goes on in many homes: sitting with a child and looking at a book; pointing to pictures and asking questions; reading a few lines, and letting the child fill in the rest; letting the child retell a familiar story. All these activities enhance the reading process, and can take place in any language. Too often, the most frequent kind of verbalization consists of commands or instructions: *close the door, watch your sister, time to eat.* Children are exposed to more advanced vocabulary, structure, and logic when listening to their elders discuss something, or when observing traditional rituals in the home or community. While parents do not necessarily have to speak more English at home, they can *expect* their children to learn both Hmong and English well.

The school is often not directly involved in Hmong community activities, but school personnel can advise and influence community leaders in the awareness of what is important to successful school achievement, the advantages of proficiency in the home language as well as the majority language, the skills and attitudes that teachers take for granted. Schools can assist communities with the organization and implementation of literacy or cultural classes, production of a community newsletter in Hmong, bringing community members into the school setting to share information with non-Hmong, and cooperation with Hmong community groups who promote skills in Hmong language and culture.

As more and more children are American born, and as the second, bilingual or bridge, generation has children, students may have been exposed to English from the beginning at home. Schools can make students and parents aware of the benefits of bilingual proficiency, and encourage children to learn the home language of their parents through auxiliary classes. A key to this is to avoid making English proficiency the only means of gaining prestige; finding ways to enhance the prestige of Hmong in the majority community will encourage children to learn and use Hmong.

❖Promoting Bilingualism and Biliteracy

Research on students of many language backgrounds strongly supports an affirmative effort by the school to cultivate each student's potential bilinguality. This approach will have rewards not only for Hmong skill levels but also for English skills levels and academic achievement .

California school personnel who wish to provide Hmong language development to Hmong-speaking students faces several obstacles related to the relative recency of a written language and the interim lack of trained teachers. The Hmong in America, however, have new materials appearing every year, due to the interest that researchers and program developers have taken in the Hmong. The school can look to the home, church, and community for literate adults and teens who can assist with Hmong literacy. University and resource centers specializing Hmong materials can provide the contacts for buying Hmong language reading materials. Schools can promote the community efforts by making available school sites for after-school literacy classes. Parent education programs in schools can share the parenting techniques that literate parents use with their young children to promote the attitudes and the prerequisite skills necessary for literacy. School personnel can help parents understand the effects of parental expectations, and encourage them to expect children to be bilingual and biliterate. Above all, the public school educators can create an atmosphere in which being bilingual and biliterate is admired and respected, and one in which both languages are regularly used.

❖Readiness for Reading and Writing Hmong

Five skills are necessary before reading and writing in Hmong can begin. The first two prerequisites for learning to read and write Hmong are the same visual skills and sensorimotor coordination that English-speaking children need to begin reading. These are nonlanguage-specific skills, but they are learned through the use of language, such as naming basic shapes, comparing same and different, and counting in order.

The next two required skills are a command of spoken Hmong and a knowledge of concepts by which the student can begin to understand and analyze meanings in the written language. Oral language development in Hmong can build both these skills at the same time. The fifth requisite for beginning to read and write is motivation.

Visual skills

Visual skills include recognizing basic shapes, sizes, and colors; telling whether patterns are the same or different; naming the items that are missing in a picture; and choosing the picture that is different from the others. Obviously there is a strong cultural component to the nature of the tasks children are asked to perform; they have to be personally familiar with the components of an object or a scene before knowing what is missing. Some children are rehearsed in these skills by parents before entering school; however, such experience should not be assumed, especially in a society so recently introduced to the visual world of the written page. These skills are necessary before learning to reading in either Hmong or English.

Sensorimotor skills

The motor control skills and eye-hand coordination skills necessary to begin writing are called sensorimotor skills. A sequence of activities usually leads from the gross-motor level to the fine-motor level and from the three-dimensional space around the body to the two-dimensional area of the page. First, isolated motions are mastered, such as jumping, throwing, catching, and clapping. Second, sustained sequences of actions related to a whole task are required; for example, acting out all the body motions that accompany a song or cutting and pasting pieces of paper to make a picture. Finally, the hands and fingers practice the fine skills of handling crayons, paper, and pencil. Prewriting pencil-and-paper practice may include drawing lines through a maze, drawing basic shapes such as circles and triangles, and making Xs or Os on work sheets in response to visual discrimination tasks. Materials that focus on prereading skills for non-native speakers are difficult to find, and native English teachers find it difficult to isolate the specific skills that need to be taught. Material developed for language delayed students often have the sequences well defined and do not assume any prior knowledge of either the concepts or the skills.

Auditory and oral language skills

Students need personal mastery of most of the sounds, syntax, and common vocabulary of spoken Hmong before they can begin to read and write. The complexity of the initial consonants of Hmong require increasingly fine auditory discrimination skills, much in the same way that English speaking children gradually develop the skill to discriminate and produce *rabbit* and *wabbit*. Young Hmong children often say *iv* rather than *txiv* ('father'); adults in the home model and expect better pronunciation as the child matures. A Hmong student must be able to discriminate and produce accurately the seven distinctive tones of the language; as with the consonant or vowel sounds, parents require more correct pronunciation as the child matures, often joking about the confusions in meaning that results from mispronounced tones. Traditional learning strategies emphasize the skills required for success in a society that does not rely on the written page, such as auditory memory skills. Students raised in Hmong speaking environments will learn these skills through daily exposure to adults who rehearse prerequisite skills in the same way that literate parents rehearse prerequuisite visual discrimination and memory skills.

Implications for Educators:

Teachers and school specialists should not overlook the possibility of untreated ear infection, or residual ear damage from previous untreated ear infections.

There are different styles of spoken Hmong, from ritual texts that contain words and phrases that are not generally understood, to interaction between siblings as they play. There appear to be regional and even lineage differences in the vocabulary and usage in rituals, and as the rituals are less often performed, the children receive less exposure to these oral language development experiences. At the same time, as Hmong from different lineage groups and dialect groups, and from different regions come to live with and interact with each other, they begin to understand and accept previously unfamiliar words and pronunciations, and the differences may be expected gradually to level out.

Implications for Educators:

Dialect differences should be considered in designing a Hmong literacy program. Most of the available written materials reflect White Hmong in their spellings and choice of words, although intended for use by all Hmong. Other materials have been written to correspond to Green Hmong dialect where pronunciations differ. (These materials will spell the word *Hmong* as 'Moob' instead of 'Hmoob'.) Just as American, Canadian, and English children can read the same books with little difficulty even though they will pronounce words differently, so if handled properly any of the Hmong materials could be used with children speaking either dialect, but allowances would need to be made. Since one factor in the choice is community makeup and preferences, schools should involve the parent community in making the decision.

Conceptual skills

Conceptual skills include the abilities to organize thoughts in chronological or thematic order, to anticipate consequences, to explain similarities and differences, to classify things, to give simple definitions, and to identify difficult words or phenomena. Development of these skills involves building awareness of surroundings, feelings, people's roles and relations, and many life experiences. As students practice these analytical skills through play, word games, and informal discussions, they prepare themselves for the conceptual demands of reading and writing.

Implications for Educators:

Folk tales and stories from different cultures have different formats and thus differences in the way that "what comes next" is anticipated. For example, in a Hmong story, the sequence appears to move from one set of characters to another, without returning in a circular manner to the characters first encountered. If *Three Little Pigs* was a Hmong story, a listener would expect the pigs to encounter a bear, and then a snake, a bird, a Chinese slave, or ants after the big, bad wolf. The student raised with European style stories is left with a sense of "what happened to the wolf?"

Motivation for reading and writing

Motivation to read and write in Hmong at school can be promoted through an environment that is rich in opportunities, reading materials, and encouragement from all teachers and students. The teachers and the principal of the school must communicate clearly the goals of the school program to the students' parents. In addition, school personnel should coordinate their efforts with those of the staffs of other Hmong literacy classes, so that the programs support each other.

It is the scarcity of good dictionaries, in particular, that leaves secondary students wondering why they should bother to learn to read Hmong. Hmong students currently in school are perhaps the first and last generation of American Hmong who could have the skills in both languages to be effective at writing and preserving the language. To some degree, encouraging and teaching Hmong literacy to this generation is an investment for future generations of Hmong, who, like other immigrant groups, will want to "find their roots", including learning to read and write the language of their grandparents.

Because so many of the initial reading materials have been developed by Christian missionary groups, it may be that Hmong who attend church regularly see more reason to read Hmong, and in fact, get more practice in reading. For those Hmong who are not Christian, the public schools may be the only place in which they have the opportunity to become literate in Hmong, and in which there is not a strong link between conversion to Christianity and learning to read.

❖Transfer of Literacy Skills

There are skills that transfer from literacy in a first language to other subsequent languages. This transfer of skills makes the learning of the second language more efficient.

The prereading skills do not have to be relearned; they are non-language specific. Students will understand that a written language is a code, and there are particular rules for decoding (reading) and encoding (writing). They will understand that the written language differs from the spoken language, but that there are conventions to help the reader make the written passage sound as much like oral speech as possible when read aloud (periods, commas, quotation marks, boldface, and so on). Literate students will have strategies for confronting a written page, and for understanding the punctuation and layout of text. They may be familiar with the physical cues that help them analyze the nature of a document (this is a letter, this is a poem, this is dialogue, and so on), even before they can fully comprehend the meaning of the words and sentences.

Literate students will know how to read for meaning in a paragraph, how to organize and classify details, how to form images of what is read. Problem solving strategies for figuring out unknown words can be applied to the second language, such as using context clues, looking just before or just after a new word to find its meaning restated, consulting a dictionary, or describing a problem that needs solving.

The surface features of written Hmong and English differ somewhat, but they are both alphabetic systems using the same roman alphabet. In addition, the concepts and purposes of reading and writing are similar in both languages. Ada (1980) divides reading skills into the four categories of readiness, decoding, comprehension, and critical reading, and shows that "no one learns to read twice.".

Community Literacy Programs

Up to the present time most teaching of Hmong reading has been done on a one-to-one basis. This method has proven highly successful, as evidenced by the many formerly illiterate Hmong adults in the United States who are now able to read and write in Hmong. Many Hmong adults have no previous classroom experience and have some difficulty learning in that type of environment. One-to-one teaching, which allows for individualized pacing, built-in tutoring, individual encouragement, and social interaction, is probably the teaching method most likely to succeed, especially for Hmong adults and elders.

There currently exists a beginning Hmong reading text published in Thailand, called *Phau Xyaum Nyeem Ntawv Hmoob*, which has been successfully used by many Hmong individuals to learn to read Hmong (Bertrais, n.d.)[7]. This small and relatively inexpensive text can be worked through within a matter of days by any person who speaks Hmong and can read the roman alphabet. Upon completion, the person will be able to read most basic Hmong words and texts.

Another White Hmong primer and reader series produced in Laos, *Kawm Ntawv Hmoob, Phau 1, Phau 2, and Tsav Nyiam Kawm Ntawv* (*Kawm Ntawv Hmoob*, n.d.), uses a sight word approach to learning Hmong. It begins with a word and its classifier, and adds words page by page until the reader can master phrases, sentences, and blocks of text. Sidebars provide minimal pairs for practicing vowel, consonant, and tone contrasts. Neither primer uses consistent capitalization or punctuation, possibly a carryover from Lao.

A primer for Green Hmong has been developed by the Mong Volunteer Literacy Group in Illinois titled *Kawm Ntawv Moob*. (Xyooj X. N., 1981). One letter/sound is presented on each page, along with five numbers. The method used is essentially sight word, or rote memorization, leading to recognition of patterns of sounds and spellings. Letters are presented in alphabetical order; the authors presume recognition of vowel and tone symbols before beginning page one. There are several small books of customs, folktales, and proverbs that follow the primer.

---

[7]This primer has appeared in several different forms, with slightly different titles, dates, and publishers/printers. They all appear to be versions of the original *Nyeem Ntawv Hmoob/Abécédaire Hmong*, by Yves Bertrais. The date of the original is unknown, but there was a Bangkok reprint available with the date 1974 (year of Buddha 2521) in Thai on the back cover (*Phau Xyaum Nyeem Ntawv Hmoob*, 1974).

A Denver group produced a primer for White Hmong, titled, *Phau Qhia Nyeem Tsiaj Ntawv Hmoob* (Xyooj T., 1981). On each page a letter is presented, with several words that are use the target letter(s). After several pages, the words are chosen to make sense, as a phrase or sentence. Unfortunately, each word is written with a capitalized first letter, regardless of its position in a sentence. Since the Hmong language has been a written language for only a relatively short time (about 40 years), there is a consequent lack of Hmong literature and/or resources for literate Hmong students to read. However, there are a few texts available in the Hmong language; they are listed in the Bibliography. As time passes, no doubt others will contribute to the limited amounts of Hmong literature.

❖Using the Phonic Method to Teach Hmong

In Hmong orthography the letters have a very consistent correspondence to the sound system, and so, the phonic method is the most effective way for teaching most students. Reading by the phonic method requires knowledge of the letter-sound correspondence and blending skills.

The pattern used to decode words is 1) produce the vowel sound on a mid tone; 2) blend the initial and the vowel on a mid tone; 3) apply the appropriate tone pattern. Thus, it goes like this: *a--pa--paj*. This pattern is practiced over and over as the letter-sound correspondence is memorized by using vowel charts (*a--pa--paj; e--pe--pej; w--pw--pw*). A regular sequence of vowels helps the memorization, as a mnenomic device; whatever sequence of vowels is chosen, it should be followed throughout the learning process.

Learning to read with fluency in school in Laos or Thailand depended on practicing or memorizing set texts of material, to be read in front of the class. This may have been a carry-over from learning in Lao schools, or may have been necessary because of the lack of books and paper. Memorization and recitation were supplemented by dictation, and eventually, sight recognition of words occured. The immediate recognition of words, rather than decoding them in a low voice and listening to the words, is essential for speed, comprehension, and the editing skills required by writing.

❖Learning to Write Hmong

Learning to write Hmong seems to be somewhat more difficult than learning to read, especially for Hmong adults and elders. This may be due to the complete lack of scholarly and literary activities in traditional Hmong life. Even holding a pencil or pen is a new skill for many Hmong elders. Some older people find learning to write their name, a necessary skill for life in the United States, as much as they are willing tc master. However, with continued practice of motor skills, use of pens, pencils, and paper, Hmong children and adults can learn to write simple Hmong texts.

Learning to write Hmong is simultaneous with learning to read. In the primer *Nyeem Ntawv Hmoob* (Bertrais, n.d.) writing is practiced as the sounds and letters are learned. Manuscript is introduced first, with cursive (European style) shown on the same page.

Usually American teachers present the manuscript form first, because it is believed that this method is more suitable for young hands and fingers. Manuscript writing requires fewer hand or eye movements. The Hmong primer was probably used with a variety of learners, from young children to adults, and since books were few, as much as possible was contained on each page.

The physical skills necessary for anyone to begin writing are: 1) establishing the dominant hand; 2) learning to manipulate the pencil or pen; 3) establishing left-to-right direction; and 4) learning to position the body, hand, and paper. Initial exercises usually include practice in making basic strokes and shapes (large and small circles, vertical lines, diagonal lines, and regular spaces). Instruction in writing is begun by having students learn to write letters of the alphabet, by copying from models.

For cursive writing, learners need to have sufficient small muscle control and coordination to enable them to make the retracing, joining, and flourishes that are part of cursive writing. The essential differences between the two forms of writing are the joining of letters and the lifting of the pencil at the ends of words rather than the ends of strokes.

Conventions for written Hmong are not readily known, and the written form mimics the spoken form exactly. When punctuation is used, it is carried over from English or French. Traditionally, composition activities for students followed the "copy the form" method of learning, in which students copy texts verbatim at first, then vary the texts according to personal style. Dictation was also extensively used, writing on slates rather than paper.

There is a grammar for White Hmong, written in French and Hmong (*Elements de Grammaire Hmong Blanc*, Mottin, 1979), and one written for Green Hmong by Thomas Lyman (1979).[8] Grammatical

---

[8]Lyman developed a different orthography, which uses diacritical marks similar to Vietnamese and different combinations of letters for Hmong sounds; this grammar, which is difficult to locate, would require learning a new

sketches of Hmong have been produced by the Center for Applied Linguistics (1978), and by advanced students of linguistics (Beckwith, n.d.; Berman, 1983), and particular aspects of Hmong grammar have been investigated in recent theses and doctoral dissertations (e.g., Ratliff, 1986; Fuller, 1985). Professor Charles Li of the University of California at Santa Barbara is currently at work on a functional reference grammar for Green Hmong.

As Hmong write for publication, issues regarding standard conventions resurface, and are handled differently by different authors. One problem concerns whether or not to write the syllables of Hmong as independent words (*kwv tij*), as compounds (*kwvtij*), or with hyphens (*kwv-tij*), even in cases where it is not possible for the syllables to exist as independent words. Another problem is how to write words that exhibit tone change when preceded by words with dominant or strong tones. In English, there is a written standard, that may differ when spoken; one writes *data* or *either* but the actual pronunciation differs from region to region, or from speaker to speaker. For Hmong there is no established standard, so writers encode what they hear, resulting in the same word spelled in different ways by different writers.

Among the younger groups of Hmong, there are a fair number who are fond of writing. Like all aspiring authors, they need a forum through which they can publish their works. Interested school or community people could assist the Hmong to find funds, volunteers, and personnel to produce journals, books, articles, and so on, in the Hmong language. This endeavor would provide two benefits, one being a way to encourage persons to write in Hmong, and the other being the provision to the Hmong and the greater community of much-needed Hmong written resources. An additional benefit is the involvement of community elders in meaningful school-home pursuits, the preservation of what they know.

Language Programs in the Schools

❖Oral Language

In California, most language minority students enter one of four types of classroom situations: 1) *grammar-based English as a Second Language* (taught as high school foreign languages are taught, with

---

orthography.

emphasis on translation, phonology, and rules); 2) *submersion* (taught as if every one is a native speaker of English); 3) *communicative-based ESL* (with emphasis on language use and language functions, the "natural approach"); or 4) *sheltered-English* (in which the subject matter is taught in English, with modified materials and special techniques that enhance comprehension). The research suggests that communicative-based ESL and sheltered English instruction best promote the acquisition of English, and the other two methods are less effective (Krashen, 1981; Terrell, 1981).

Depending on the age of the student entering the American schools, and the school environment, appropriate program design will differ. The basic guideline to remember is that language acquisition takes place when the input is made comprehensible in some way (whether by using pictures, hand signals, "motherese", modified materials, bilingual aides, or peer tutors). Young children who enter school at kindergarten find an environment that provides plenty of comprehensible input; kindergarten teachers use short phrases, demonstrations, repetition, and instructions to perform physical activities. On the other hand, high school teachers use English that has fewer apparent clues as to meaning, and students cannot watch and mimic peers as kindergarteners do.

Grammar-based ESL classes are usually offer one of two approaches: grammar-translation (inductive), or audiolingual or cognitive code (deductive) methods. Either of these approaches leads to the development of a language monitor (Krashen, 1981). The monitor assists learners of English in producing carefully constructed and grammatically accurate utterances. Before the monitor can be effectively used, the task at hand must be focused on language forms in some way (for example, a grammar test); the students must have already learned the grammar rule; they must recognize the appropriateness of the situation for the rule; and they need sufficient time to retrieve the rule, adapt it to the situation, and use it correctly in producing an utterance. Seldom does the normal speech situation allow for these conditions. The monitor can actually inhibit the output of language.

In submersion environments language minority students are placed with native English speaking peers and a native English teacher who teaches as though there are only native English speakers in the room. Submersion environments are less effective than grammar-based ESL classes, because during submersion lessons, the students do not comprehend much of what is said. Krashen (1981) states that the critical elements of "comprehensible input" are 1) what the student can already comprehend, and 2) the additional input that is made comprehensible by a variety of techniques. In submersion classes, there is too much input that is too far removed from the level of comprehension of the student. Cummins (1981) and Krashen (1981) have conducted research that shows that in submersion environments, neither the ability to communicate socially nor the cognitive/academic skills are developed.

Language skills in English, both the interpersonal communicative skills and the underlying cognitive/academic language proficiency, are most successfully acquired when students are placed in either communicative-based ESL (the natural approach), or sheltered English classes. After the student developes intermediate language skills, grammar-based ESL or submersion may be appropriate.

❖Literacy in Two Languages

The appropriate time to introduce reading instruction depends on the goals of the program. If the goal is biliteracy, then reading instruction would begin in Hmong, in kindergarten and continue through at least sixth grade. Formal instruction in English reading would begin at about second or third grade, after the basic processes are strongly developed in the primary language, including higher reading skills such as inference and study skills. In transitional bilingual programs, reading instruction is begun in the primary language and is continued until about 4th grade, when a transition is made to reading only in English. In English-only programs, students attain the readiness skills necessary for reading instruction, and begin to read in English. Essential readiness skills would be interpersonal communicative skills and underlying cognitive skills demonstrated by native English speakers when they begin reading instruction.

There are four basic choices in organizing a reading program in bilingual contexts:

- •Begin literacy in Hmong, introduce English later, at second or third grade; continue both through sixth grade.
- •Simultaneous instruction in both Hmong and English.
- •Begin literacy in English then teach Hmong literacy (immersion programs).
- •Literacy instruction in English only.

Hmong followed by English

When there are sufficient human and material resources available and the parents support the concept, the first-language reading approach appears to be effective in developing full bilingualism and biliteracy, with fully developed cognitive and academic skills

92

(Cummins, 1981). An effective program introduces reading in the primary language in the first grade and continues it until third grade. Formal English reading instruction begins in third grade, and instruction in both languages is continued to sixth grade (Rosier and Holm, 1980; Cummins, 1981). The effects of reading instruction are cumulative, adding up year after year, and the best results are achieved after a seven year program (Cummins, 1981). Proficient bilingual and biliterate students have definite advantages over other language minority students and even over monolingual students (Cummins, 1981; Kessler and Quinn, 1980; *Evaluation of California's Education Services*, 1981).

Hmong and English simultaneously

In these programs, students learn to read in Hmong and English at the same time. Some studies suggest that there is confusion (like "false cognates") when learning two alphabetic systems at the same time, that is not a problem when learning characters (like Chinese) and letters (like English) at the same time. The confusion arises when the letters represent different sounds or follow different rules in the two coding systems; for example *q* in Hmong (*qeej*) does not take a *u* after it, nor does it represent the same sound as it does in English.

The key to an effective program would be the coordination between the lessons and teaching staff of the two reading programs. It would not be necessary to teach twice the underlying skills that are developed by reading instruction (for example, a student learns to alphabetize only once). If one teacher teaches both languages, it has been shown to be more effective if the instruction periods are clearly separated in terms of time, materials, and environment. Simultaneous literacy instruction does not mean mixing the two languages in the same activity. Rather, it should involve complementing and enhancing the student's literacy development through the use of two languages in separate, efficient, challenging sets of activites.

English followed by Hmong (immersion programs)

Immersion programs in French for native English speaking students have been in operation in Canada for more than a decade, and there have been several experimental programs in the U.S. In these programs, all instruction is given in the students' second language (for example, English), including literacy instruction (in the language of immersion, English). At second or third grade, language arts instruction in the primary language (French) is begun. Research has shown that most students in French immersion programs achieve high levels of literacy in both languages (Cummins, 1981; Krashen, 1981; Genessee, 1980; *Studies on Immersion Education*, 1984). Even though students were provided with most of their instruction in French, once English language arts were added to the curriculum, the students quickly caught up to their monolingually schooled peers. In fact, the students in the immersion program did as well in English reading as did the students in English-only programs (Genesee, 1980). In addition, the students were proficient in French.

One should note that the immersion programs are especially designed so that native English-speaking students acquire a second language while at the same time experiencing normal academic and English development. These students, in general, attain a level of proficient bilingualism. Implementing such programs in the U.S. should be based on a commitment by educators to promote the LEP students' academic learning as well as comparable proficiency in both English and their native language.

English only

For a variety of reasons--philosophical position, desires of the students and parents, or lack of educational resources--some school districts will continue to provide Hmong students with English-only, submersion type reading instruction. Fortunately, most programs offer at least oral ESL instruction; nevertheless, few recognized ESL (initial) literacy curricula are available; and few staff members are trained in this approach. Unfortunately, most of the activities in the ESL program tend to be remedial versions of the same activities used with native English speakers.

Under the best circumstances within the English-only option, formal English reading instruction should be delayed until language minority students have acquired some basic interpersonal communicative skills in English. Once an oral language base in English is established, students will be better able to cope with the more cognitively demanding concepts associated with literacy. Educators should be aware that since Hmong literacy is not addressed, a subtractive form of bilingualism will probably be the result for most students.

Clearly, English-only reading instruction is not a recommended option. However, if such an option is used, there are several suggestions for making it the best possible program:

1. Provide students with ample amounts of comprehensible input in English, so that basic communicative skills will be acquired.
2. Provide cognitive/academic language development through sheltered English strategies.
3. Group second language students apart from native speakers for part of the oral language and literacy development, where communicative ESL and sheltered English strategies can be employed.
4. Sequence instruction appropriately so that students will not be introduced to the new concepts until they have acquired the appropriate linguistic and academic background sufficient for more complex skills.
5. Analyze English reading materials in order to anticipate where the students may have difficulty with vocabulary, syntax, and cultural content.
6. Provide interested parents with materials and instructions to carry out language tasks at home in Hmong. Teachers should encourage parents to focus on activities that better prepare students for the academic requirements of school.
7. Teach students strategies for coping with unfamiliar materials, and study skills for researching unknown concepts, use library resources, and so forth.

In practice, few programs will have biliteracy in Hmong and English as their goals; the resources, methodology, and trained teachers are too few to implement such programs, and the parents, who grew up in multilingual societies, place an emphasis on early learning of the majority language. Biliteracy will produce positive outcomes, and schools can foster Hmong literacy by encouraging and assisting the Hmong community in efforts to conduct classes in literacy, produce materials to read, and training teachers who are bilingual and biliterate. However, appropriate school instruction must consider the negative effects of limited bilingualism, in which students become semi-proficient in English, and yet are limited in their own language.

In summary, effective reading programs in bilingual contexts require that school personnel correctly match the instructional approach with student needs, community desires, and human and material resources. Regardless of the approach selected, the quality of implementation is the key to producing positive outcomes. In practical terms, for Hmong students, acquiring English skills in understanding, speaking, reading, and writing should be combined with, at least, effective re-instruction of key concepts and vocabulary in Hmong. This will enhance the development of underlying cognitive/academic skills, as well as promoting the ability to reason and speak in Hmong. Practical activities, that are fairly easy to implement with the help of bilingual aides, include:

ELEMENTARY:
•Reviewing basal reading vocabulary with a Hmong aide.
•Reviewing weekly spelling words with a Hmong aide.
•Reviewing vocabulary and key concepts in science and social science with a Hmong aide.

SECONDARY:
•Sheltered English courses in the core requirements that use simplified, vocabulary based English materials and re-instruction or review with a Hmong aide/teacher.

As the training and certification of bilingual teachers becomes a reality, more options for effective programs will be possible.

Historically, parents and educators have considered the acquisition of interpersonal communication skills the only goal for language minority students. However, having sufficient language skills with which to reason, think, and learn are important to school success. The danger facing language minority students who are new to the United States is that they will be limited in both languages. While full biliteracy is the optimal goal, the reality is that designing public school programs to attain that goal is very difficult if not impossible. Hmong children come from a heritage of multilingualism; parents know that to succeed in a country, one has to be very good at the majority language, while within each ethnic group, people speak to one another in their own language. The maintenance of the Hmong language is important to the continuity of ethnic identity, and does not exclude a desire for knowing English well.

Most Hmong parents also come from a background that did not include school as part of everyone's experience. Programs for Hmong children, then, will be made more effective as the parents are educated in the processes and underlying beliefs of the American school systems. Parents will benefit from knowing how native-born parents of successful students interact with their children from the earliest age.

Schools who have Hmong children can provide appropriate programs for children by keeping in mind these guidelines:

1. To acquire a language (English or Hmong), children must be exposed to it, the input must be comprehensible, and there must be a positive attitude towards acquiring it.
2. To succeed in school, underlying cognitive language skills are necessary, in at least one language.

96

3. There are ways in which parents can increase their children's chances for academic success, and schools can teach parents these skills.
4. There are ways for schools to incorporate the use of Hmong in programs which emphasize English, even though there are currently inadequate/insufficient Hmong materials and personnel.
5. Schools can work cooperatively with Hmong community groups to plan and implement Hmong literacy and culture classes outside of the regular school day.
6. School programs must be flexible enough to meet the changing needs of the incoming Hmong populations.

Language development, oral and written, in English and/or the native language, forms only one of many components of an appropriate and effective educational program for Hmong students. Other components include strong academic content, psychosocial support, staff development, school climate, home-school relations, parent education programs, and vocational/college counseling.

Bibliography

❖References

Ada, Alma Flor. 1980. "No One Learns to Read Twice: The Transferability of Reading Skills."*Aids to Bilingual Education Report* (6).

Barney, G. Linwood, and William A. Smalley. 1953. "Third Report on Meo (Miao): Orthography and Grammar." Mimeo.

Beckwith, Judith Mazur. No date. "A Preliminary Description of Hmong." Seminar Paper No. 49. Department of Linguistics, California State University, Fullerton.

Benedict, Paul K. 1985. "Early Sino-Tibetan/Hmong-Mien Loan Relationships" Paper presented at the SEASSI Conference, Ann Arbor, 1-3 August. (Forthcoming in *Linguistics of the Tibeto-Burman Area*.)

Berman, Judith. 1983. "A Preliminary Sketch of Hmong Phonology, Grammar, and Syntax. Part One: Phonology. Part Two: Morphology, Grammar, and Syntax." *Educational Linguistics*, University of Pennsylvania.

Bertrais, Yves. No date. *Nyeem Ntawv Hmoob*/Reading Hmong, *Abécédaire Hmong, First Steps in Hmong*. (Distributed by Association Communauté Hmong, French Guiana.) [Also published as: *Nyeem Ntawv Hmoob, Hmong Primer/Abécédaire Hmong/First Steps in Hmong.*. Paris: Institut de L'Asie du Sud-Est, Rooj Ntawv Hmoob; *Phau Xyaum Nyeem Ntawv Hmoob*. 1974. Bangkok: Rooj Ntawv Hmoob.]

-----------. 1985-87. *Collection "Patrimoine Culturel Hmong"*. (Consists of 8 works, completed and in preparation.) French Guiana: Association Communauté Hmong. [Includes these titles: *Kab Ke Pam Tuag: Cov Zaj*/Funeral Ceremonies: Songs and Recitations (1987); *Keeb Kwm Hmoob Raws Tsev Koom Haum Vib Nais*/Origin of the Hmong, according to Vinai Confraternity (1985); *Dab Neeg: Phau Ib*/Tales and Legends, Book 1 (1985); *Cim Xeeb Haav Txiv Daw*/Memoir of the Green Hmong of Anning , China (1985); *Kab Tshoob Kev Kos: Phau Ib.*/Marriage Rites, Book 1 (1985); *Xyum Nyeem Ntawv Hmoob Ntsuab.*/Practice Reading Green Hmong (1985); *Kab Ke Pam Tuag: Cov Txheej Txheem*/Funeral Rituals (in preparation); *Dab Neeg Phau Ob*/Tales and Legends, Book 2 (in preparation).]

Berval, René de. 1959. *Kingdom of Laos.* Limoges, France: A. Bontemps Co., Ltd.

Bessac, Suzanne L. 1982. "The Significance of a New Script for the Hmong." Unpublished manuscript.

Chindarsi, Nusit. 1976. *The Religion of the Hmong Njua.* Bangkok, Thailand: The Siam Society.

Cummins, J. 1981. "The Role of Primary Language Development in Promoting Educational Success for Language Minority Students" In *Schooling and Language Minority Students: A Theoretical Framework.* Developed by the California State Department of Education; Office of Bilingual Bicultural Education. Los Angeles: Evaluation, Dissemination and Assessment Center, California State University, Los Angeles.

de Beauclair, Inez. 1970. "A Miao Tribe of Southeast Kweichow and its Cultural Configuration." In Inez de Beauclair, *Tribal Cultures of Southeast Asia.* Asian Folklore and Social Life Monographs (II). Taipei, Taiwan: The Orient Cultural Service.

Downing, Bruce T., Timothy Dunnigan, and William A. Smalley. No date. Manuscript. *The Hmong in America: Tradition and Adaptation in Language, Communication, and Social Organization.*

Downing, Bruce T., and Judith Wheaton Fuller. 1985. "Hmong Names: Change and Variation in a Bilingual Context." In *Papers from the 10th Minnesota Regional Conference on Language and Linguistics, May 11-12.* Edited by Nancy Stenson. *Minnesota Papers in Linguistics and Philosophy of Language 10: 39-50.*

Downing, Bruce T., and Douglas P. Olney, editors. 1982. *The Hmong in the West: Observations and Reports.* Minneapolis: Center for Urban Regional Affairs, University of Minnesota.

Dunnigan, Timothy. 1982. "Segmentary Kinship in an Urban Society: The Hmong of St. Paul-Minneapolis." *Anthropological Quarterly 55(3): 126-136.*

Dwyer, Sharon. 1982. "An Error Analysis of English Compositions Written by Hmong College Students." In *The Hmong in the West: Observations and Reports.* Edited by Bruce T. Downing and Douglas P. Olney. Minneapolis: Center for Urban Regional Affairs, University of Minnesota, pp. 226-248.

Evaluation of California's Educational Services to Limited- and Non-English-Speaking Students, Final Report. 1981. San Francisco: Development Associates, Inc.

Fuller, Judith Wheaton. 1985. *Topic and Comment in Hmong.* Ph.D.

dissertation, University of Minnesota.

Genesee, F. 1980. "Acquisition of Reading Skills in Immersion Programs." *Foreign Language Annals (February)*.

Green, Karen Reed, and Stephen Reder. 1986. "Factors in Individual Acquisition of English: A Longitudinal Study of Hmong Adults." In *The Hmong in Transition*. Edited by Glenn L. Hendricks, Bruce T. Downing, and Amos S. Deinard. New York: Center for Migration Studies, pp. 299-329.

Greenberg, Joseph. 1953. "Historical Linguistics and Unwritten Languages." In *Anthropology Today*. Edited by A.L. Kroeber. Chicago: University of Chicago Press.

Haiv Hmoob/Hmong Magazine. 1985-. (Yang, Dao, editor. P.O. Box 11314, Minneapolis, MN 55411).

Heimbach, Ernest E. 1979. *White Hmong-English Dictionary. Data Paper Number 75*. Ithaca, New York: Cornell University, Southeast Asia Program.

Hendricks, Glenn L., Bruce T. Downing, and Amos S. Deinard, editors. 1986. *The Hmong in Transition*. New York: Center for Migration Studies.

The Hmong World (1). 1986. Edited by Brenda Johns and David Strecker. New Haven, CT: Council on Southeast Asia Studies. Yale Center for International & Area Studies.

Jarkey, Nerida. 1985a. "Consonant Phonemes of White Hmong." Manuscript.

----------. 1985 b. "Vowel Phonemes of White Hmong." Manuscript.

Kawm Ntawv Hmoob, Phau 1/Learn Hmong, book 1. No date. Ntawv Hmoob.

Kawm Ntawv Hmoob, Phau 2/Learn Hmong, book 2. No date. Ntawv Hmoob.

Kessler, C., and M. Quinn. 1980. "Bilingualism and Science Problem-Solving Ability." *Bilingual Education Paper Series 4(1) August*. Los Angeles: National Dissemination and Assessment Center, California State University, Los Angeles.

Krashen, S. 1981. "Bilingual Education and Second Language Acquisition Theory." In *Schooling and Language Minority Students: A Theoretical Framework*. Developed by the California State Department of Education; Office of Bilingual Bicultural Education. Los Angeles: Evaluation, Dissemination and Assessment Center, California State University, Los Angeles.

Lartéguy, Jean, and Dao Yang. 1978. *La Fabuleuse Aventure du Peuple de l'Opium*. Paris: Presses de la Cité.

Lee, Gary Yia. 1982. "National Minority Policy and the Hmong." In *Contemporary Laos*, edited by Martin Stuart-Fox. New York: St. Martin's Press, pp. 199-219.

Lemoine, Jacques. 1972. "Les écritures du Hmong"/Hmong writing systems. *Bulletin des Amis du Royaume Lao (Vientiane) 7-8:123-165*.

Lis Nyiajpov. 1985. *Vim Leejtwg*/Whose Fault? Bonnyrigg, Australia: Roojntawv Neejmhoob.

----------. 1986. *Lub Neej Daitaw*/A Marginal Life. Bonnyrigg, Australia: Roojntawv Neejmhoob.

----------. 1987. *Txoj Sawlhub*/The Necklace of Love. Bonnyrigg, Australia: Roojntawv Neejmhoob.

----------. **forthcoming**. *Esxias Thaum Ncaim*/When Leaving Asia. Bonnyrigg, Australia: Roojntawv Neejmhoob.

----------. **forthcoming**. *Lub Neej Kuamuag*/The Life of Tears. Bonnyrigg, Australia: Roojntawv Neejmhoob

Lyman, Thomas A. 1974. *Dictionary of Mong Njua (Green Miao), A Miao (Meo) Language of Southeast Asia*. The Hague: Mouton; Walter de Gruyter Distributors.

----------. 1979. *Grammar of Mong Njua*. Published by the author. [Forthcoming new edition from Sattley, CA: The Blue Oak Press.]

Malcolm, Lois, 1983. "Hmong Bilinguals: How Did They Learn English?" *MinneTESOL Journal 3:29-41*.

Minnesota Governor's Advisory Council for Refugees Thailand Trip Report, December, 1986.

Mottin, Jean. 1978. *Elements de Grammaire Hmong Blanc*/Elements of White Hmong Grammar. Bangkok, Thailand: Don Bosco Press.

National Indochinese Clearinghouse. 1978. *The Hmong Language: Sounds and Alphabets*. Indochinese Refugee Education Guides, General Information Series #14. Arlington, Virginia: Center for Applied Linguistics. (ERIC #AD157 400).

National Indochinese Clearinghouse. 1978. *The Hmong Language: Sentences, Phrases, and Words*. Indochinese Refugee Education Guides, General Information Series #15. Arlington, Virginia: Center for Applied Linguistics. (ERIC #AD158 592).

National Indochinese Clearinghouse. 1980. *English Pronunciation Lessons for Hmongs.* Indochinese Refugee Education Guides, General Information Series #21. Arlington, Virginia: Center for Applied Linguistics. (ERIC #AD188 498).

Owensby, Laurel. 1986. "Verb Serialization in Hmong." In *The Hmong in Transition,* Edited by Glenn L. Hendricks, Bruce T. Downing, and Amos S. Deinard. New York: Center for Migration Studies.

Pollard, Sam. 1919. *The Story of the Miao.* London: Henry Hooks.

Ratliff, Martha Susan. 1986. *The Morphological Functions of Tone in White Hmong.* Ph.D. dissertation, University of Chicago.

Reder, Stephen. 1982. "A Hmong Community's Acquisition of English." In *The Hmong in the West: Observations and Reports.* Edited by Bruce T. Downing and Douglas P. Olney. Minneapolis: Center for Urban Regional Affairs, University of Minnesota, pp. 268-303.

Reder, Stephen, Karen Reed Green, and Michael P. Sweeney. 1983. *Acquisition and Use of Literacy in the Hmong Community of Newton: 1981 Annual Report of the Functional Literacy Project.* Portland, Oregon: Northwest Regional Laboratory.

Roberts, T.D., et al. 1966. *Area Handbook for Laos.* Washington, D.C.: Superintendent of Documents, U.S. Government Printing Office.

Rosier, P., and W. Holm. 1980. "The Rock Point Experience: A Longitudinal Study of a Navajo School (Saad Naaki Bee N'nitin)." *Bilingual Education Series No. 8.* Arlington, VA: Center for Applied Linguistics.

Ruhlen, Merritt. 1976. *A Guide to Languages of the World.* Stanford, California: Merritt Ruhlen.

Schooling and Language Minority Students: A Theoretical Framework. 1981. Developed by the California State Department of Education; Office of Bilingual Bicultural Education. Los Angeles: Evaluation, Dissemination and Assessment Center, California State University, Los Angeles.

Smalley, William A. 1985. "Adaptive Language Strategies of the Hmong: From Asian Mountains to American Ghettos." *Language Sciences 7(2): 241-269.*

----------. 1986. "Stages of Hmong Cultural Adaptation." In *The Hmong in Transition.* Edited by Glenn L. Hendricks, Bruce T. Downing, and Amos S. Deinard. New York: Center for Migration Studies, pp. 7-22.

Spring 1987 Language Census Survey, Data Bical Report No. 87-8N (Fall). 1987. Sacramento, CA: California State Department of Education.

State Science Framework. 1984. Sacramento, CA: State Department of Education.

Strecker, David. 1981. "A Preliminary Note on the Classification and Terminology of the Hmongic (Miao) Languages." Unpublished paper.

----------. 1984. Letter to Douglas P. Olney, January 27.

Studies on Immersion Education. 1984. Sacramento: California State Department of Education.

Terrell, T. 1981. "The Natural Approach in Bilingual Education." In *Schooling and Language Minority Students: A Theoretical Framework*. Developed by the California State Department of Education; Office of Bilingual Bicultural Education. Los Angeles: Evaluation, Dissemination and Assessment Center, California State University, Los Angeles.

Thao, Cheu. 1981. *English-Hmong Phrasebook with Useful Wordlist*. Washington, D.C.: Center for Applied Linguistics.

Tsav Nyiam Kawm Ntawv/Ja Likes to Study. No date. Ntawv Hmoob. Follows Book 1 and 2.

Vajtswv tej lus uas cawm neeg txojsia/Bible. 1981. Bangkok: The Bible Society of Thailand.

Vang, Gaohli Lyfoung. 1983. *Phau Nkauj Yexus Khetos*/Hmong Hymnal. Rockford, Illinois: Hmong Valley Baptist Church.

Vang, Lue, and Judy Lewis. 1984. *Grandmother's Path, Grandfather's Way*. Rancho Cordova, CA: Zellerbach Family Fund.

Xiong, Lang, Joua Xiong, and Nao Leng Xiong. 1983. *English-Mong-English Dictionary*/Phoo Txhais Lug Aakiv-Moob-Aakiv. Milwaukee, WI: Published by the authors.

Xyooj Tsheej. 1981. *Phau Qhia Nyeem Tsiaj Ntawv Hmoob*/Book to Teach Reading the Hmong Alphabet. Denver, CO.

Xyooj Xeev Nruag, editor. 1981. *Kawm Ntawv Moob*/Learn (Green) Hmong. Wheaton, IL: Mong Voluntary Literacy Group.

----------. 1984. *Kawm Ntawv Moob, Phoo 2*/Learn (Green) Hmong, Book 2. Wheaton, IL: Mong Voluntary Literacy International, Inc.

----------. 1984. *Phoo/Phau Kawm Koom, Moob Leeg/Hmoob Dawb*/Book to Learn Green Hmong and White Hmong Together. Wheaton, IL: Mong Voluntary Literacy Group.

----------. *Lub Nruag Moob: The Mong Popular Tales and Fables (6 titles)*.

Wheaton, IL: Mong Voluntary Literacy Group. [Includes: *Paaj Lug Moob*/Hmong Proverbs (Thoj, 1983); *Phoo Qha Siv Lu Lug Meej hab Tsi Meej*/Book that Explains How to Use Similar Words Correctly (Thoj, 1982); *Puj Dlab Has Lug Nruag Kwv Huam Kevlis Kevcai Kaabtshoob Kevkug Moob*/Stories about Courtship and Bride Price (Thoj and Thoj, 1981); *Lug Nruag Moob: Lug Nruag Dlaab*/"Ghost" Folktales (Thoj, Hawj, and Xyooj, no date); *Lug Nruag Moob: Lug Nruag Lom Zem*/Humorous Folktales (Thoj, Hawj, and Xyooj, no date); *Lug Nruag Moob: Lug Nruag Txa*/"Transformation" Folktales (Thoj, Hawj, and Xyooj, no date); *Lug Nruag Moob: Lug Nruag Tsuv*/"Tiger" Folktales (Thoj, Hawj, Vaaj, and Xyooj, no date)].

Yang, Dao. 1980. "Guerre de gaz: solution communiste des problèmes des minorités au Laos?/Gas Warfare: The Communist Solution to the Problems of the Minorities in Laos?" *Les Temps Moderne* 402 (January): 1208-1222.

------------. 1982. "Why Did the Hmong Leave Laos?" In *The Hmong in the West: Observations and Reports*. Edited by Bruce T. Downing and Douglas P. Olney. Minneapolis: Center for Urban Regional Affairs, University of Minnesota, pp. 3-18.

------------. 1984a. "The Hmong Refugees of North Laos." (In French.) *La Documentation Française* .

------------. 1984b. "Human Rights and Gas Warfare in Laos." *Southeast Asia Review 1.*

❖Recommended Readings

(General works for an introduction to the Hmong people and language.)

Dunnigan, Timothy and Douglas P. Olney. 1985. "Hmong." In *Refugees in the United States: A Reference Handbook*. Edited by David W. Haines. Westport, Connecticut, and London: Greenwood Press, pp. 111-126.

Hendricks, Glenn L., Bruce T. Downing, and Amos S. Deinard, editors. 1986. *The Hmong in Transition*. New York: Center for Migration Studies.

The Hmong World (1). 1986. Edited by Brenda Johns and David Strecker. New Haven, CT: Council on Southeast Asia Studies. Yale Center for International & Area Studies.

Kershaw, Greet 1982. "Hmong families in Long Beach 1978-82: Between Incorporation and Rejection." Unpublished paper, Department of Anthropology, California State University, Long Beach.

National Indochinese Clearinghouse. 1978. *The Hmong Language: Sounds and Alphabets.* Indochinese Refugee Education Guides, General Information Series #14. Arlington, Virginia: Center for Applied Linguistics. (ERIC #AD157 400).

National Indochinese Clearinghouse. 1978. *The Hmong Language: Sentences, Phrases, and Words.* Indochinese Refugee Education Guides, General Information Series #15. Arlington, Virginia: Center for Applied Linguistics. (ERIC #AD158 592).

National Indochinese Clearinghouse. 1978. *Glimpses of Hmong History and Culture.* Indochinese Refugee Education Guides, General Information Series #16. Arlington, Virginia: Center for Applied Linguistics. (Reprinted as *The Hmong: Their History and Culture,* 1979. Lutheran Immigration and Refugee Service.) (ERIC #AD159 901).

National Indochinese Clearinghouse. 1980. *English Pronunciation Lessons for Hmongs.* Indochinese Refugee Education Guides, General Information Series #21. Arlington, Virginia: Center for Applied Linguistics. (ERIC #AD1188 498).

Reder, Stephen, Karen Reed Green, and Michael P. Sweeney. 1983. *Acquisition and Use of Literacy in the Hmong Community of Newton: 1981 Annual Report of the Functional Literacy Project.* Portland, Oregon: Northwest Regional Laboratory.

Vang, Lue, and Judy Lewis. 1984. *Grandmother's Path, Grandfather's Way.* Rancho Cordova, CA: Zellerbach Family Fund.

❖Bilingual Hmong/English Materials and ❖Materials in the Hmong Language

Bertrais, Yves. No date. *Nyeem Ntawv Hmoob*/Reading Hmong, *Abécédaire Hmong, First Steps in Hmong.* (Distributed by Association Communauté Hmong, French Guiana.) [Also published as: *Nyeem Ntawv Hmoob, Hmong Primer/Abécédaire Hmong/First Steps in Hmong..* Paris: Institut de L'Asie du Sud-Est, Rooj Ntawv Hmoob; *Phau Xyaum Nyeem Ntawv Hmoob.* 1974. Bangkok: Rooj Ntawv Hmoob; *A E T: Phau Xyaum Nyeem Ntawv Hmoob*/Book to Practice Reading Hmong. Bangkok, Thailand: Rooj Ntawv Hmoob, 1981. (Reprinted by Minneapolis Public Schools).]

----------. 1985-87. *Collection "Patrimoine Culturel Hmong".* (Consists of 8 works, completed and in preparation.) French Guiana: Association

Communauté Hmong. [Includes these titles: *Kab Ke Pam Tuag: Cov Zaj*/Funeral Ceremonies: Songs and Recitations (1987); *Keeb Kwm Hmoob Raws Tsev Koom Haum Vib Nais*/Origin of the Hmong, according to Vinai Confraternity (1985); *Dab Neeg: Phau Ib*/Tales and Legends, Book 1 (1985); *Cim Xeeb Haav Txiv Daw*/Memoir of the Green Hmong of Anning , China (1985); *Kab Tshoob Kev Kos: Phau Ib.*/Marriage Rites, Book 1 (1985); *Xyum Nyeem Ntawv Hmoob Ntsuab.*/Practice Reading Green Hmong (1985); *Kab Ke Pam Tuag: Cov Txheej Txheem*/Funeral Rituals (in preparation); *Dab Neeg Phau Ob*/Tales and Legends, Book 2 (in preparation).]

------------. 1964. *Dictionnaire Hmong (Meo Blanc)–Français.* Vientiane: Mission Catholique.

Bertrais, Yves, and Yaj Daiv. 1974. *Kwv Txhiaj Hmoob*/Hmong Chants of Love. Summer Institute of Linguistics.

Banasik, Sandra, and Som Yej Xyooj. 1981. *Xyaum Nyeem Ntawv Hmoob.* Phau 1, 2, 3, 4/Practice Reading Hmong, Books 1, 2, 3, 4. Salem, OR: Chemeketa Community College.

Brophy, Heather St. Claire, and Nhia Khang; illustrations by Deborah Foss. 1985. *Neng Souane and the Turtle: An Activity Book* (K-3 Reading). Sacramento: Voqui & Associates (P.O. Box 254892, Sacramento, CA 95865).

------------. 1985. *The Fox and the Eagle/Tus Hma thiab Tus Dav: An Activity Book* (K-3 Reading). Sacramento: Voqui & Associates (P.O. Box 254892, Sacramento, CA 95865).

English-Hmong Lessons. No date. Minneapolis Public Schools. (Reprint of a book originally prepared in Laos or Thailand).

Haiv Hmoob/Hmong Magazine, 1985–. (Dao Yang, editor, P.O. Box 11314, Minneapolis, MN 55411).

Heimbach, Ernest E. 1979. *White Hmong-English Dictionary, Data Paper Number 75.* . Ithaca, New York: Cornell University, Southeast Asia Program. (Originally published as *White Meo-English Dictionary*, 1969).

The Hmong World (1). 1986. Edited by Brenda Johns and David Strecker. New Haven, CT: Council on Southeast Asia Studies, Yale Center for International & Area Studies.

Johnson, Charles, editor. 1985. *Dab Neeg Hmoob/Myths, Legends and Folk Tales from the Hmong of Laos.* Edited by Charles Johnson. St. Paul, MN: Linguistics Department, Macalester College.

------------. 1981. *Hmong Folk Tales* (A series of 11 titles, each at two levels of difficulty). St. Paul, MN: Linguistics Department, Macalester College.

Kawm Ntawv Hmoob, Phau 1/Learn Hmong, book 1. No date. Ntawv Hmoob.

Kawm Ntawv Hmoob, Phau 2/Learn Hmong, book 2. No date. Ntawv Hmoob.

Lauj, Xeeb thiab Nyom Yaj. 1982. *Neeg Thiab Txuj Ci*/People and Culture. Minneapolis, MN: Minneapolis Public Schools.

Lis Pov and Kong Cher Vang. 1981. *Nkauj Hmoob*/Hmong Songs. St. Paul, MN.

Lis Nyiajpov. 1986. *Lub Neej Daitaw*/A Marginal Life. Bonnyrigg, Australia: Roojntawv Neejmhoob.

----------. 1985. *Vim Leejtwg*/Whose Fault?. Bonnyrigg, Australia: Roojntawv Neejmhoob.

----------. 1987. *Txoj Sawlhub*/The Necklace of Love. Bonnyrigg, Australia: Roojntawv Neejmhoob.

----------. forthcoming. *Esxias Thaum Ncaim*/When Leaving Asia. Bonnyrigg, Australia: Roojntawv Neejmhoob.

----------. forthcoming. *Lub Neej Kuamuag*/The Life of Tears. Bonnyrigg, Australia: Roojntawv Neejmhoob.

Lyman, Thomas A. 1969. "Green Miao (Meo) Proverbs." *Asia Aakhanee*: Southeast Asian Survey, 1(2): 30-32.

----------. 1970. *English-Meo Pocket Dictionary*. Bangkok, Thailand: The German Cultural Institute.

----------. 1974. *Dictionary of Mong Njua (Green Miao), A Miao (Meo) Language of Southeast Asia*. The Hague: Mouton.

----------. 1979. *Grammar of Mong Njua (Green Miao): A Descriptive Linguistic Study*. Published by author. [Forthcoming new edition from Sattley, CA: The Blue Oak Press.]

Moody, Walter. 1967. "List of Irregularities of Correspondence Existing Between Blue and White Meo Dialects, with Texts in Blue and White Meo." (unpublished).

Mottin, Jean. 1980. *Contes et Legendes Hmong Blanc*/White Hmong Stories and Legends. Bangkok, Thailand: Don Bosco Press.

----------. 1978. *Elements de Grammaire Hmong Blanc*/Elements of White Hmong Grammar. Bangkok, Thailand: Don Bosco Press.

----------. 1980 *55 Chants D'Amour Hmong Blanc*/55 White Hmong Chants of Love. Bangkok, Thailand: Don Bosco Press.

Robson, Barbara and Cawv Thoj. 1981. *Phau Xyaum Sau Ntawv Hmoob*/Writing Workbook. Washington, D.C: Center for Applied Linguistics.

----------. 1981. *Phau Xyaum Nyeem Sau Zauv*/Reading & Writing Numbers. Washington, D.C: Center for Applied Linguistics.

Savina, F.M. 1916. *Dictionnaire miao-tseu-français*/Hmong-French Dictionary. Bulletin de l'Ecole Française d'Extreme-Orient 16(2).

----------. 1920. *Abecedaire Meo-Français*/Hmong-French Reader Hanoi: Imprimerie d'Extreme Orient.

----------. 1920. *Lexique Meo-Français*/Hmong Lexicon. Hanoi: Imprimerie d'Extreme Orient.

Strecker, David and Lopao Vang. 1986. *White Hmong Dialogues. Occasional Papers #3.* Minneapolis, MN: SE Asian Refugee Studies Project, University of Minnesota.

Thoj, Phaj. 1983. *Paaj Lug Moob*/Hmong Proverbs. Edited by Xyooj Xeev Nruag. Wheaton, IL: Mong Voluntary Literacy Group.

--------. 1982 *Phoo Qha Siv Lu Lug Meej hab Tsi Meej*/Book that Explains How to Use Similar Words Correctly. Edited by Xyooj Xeev Nruag. Wheaton, IL: Mong Voluntary Literacy Group.

Thoj, Phaj and Xeev Poj Thoj. 1981. *Puj Dlab Has Lug Nruag Kwv Huam Kevlis Kevcai Kaabtshoob Kevkug Moob*/Stories about Courtship and Bride Price. Edited by Xyooj Xeev Nruag. Wheaton, IL: Mong Voluntary Literacy Group.

Thoj, Phaj, Khu Ntxawg Hawj, and Xeev Nruag Xyooj. No date. *Lug Nruag Moob: Lug Nruag Dlaab*/"Ghost" Folktales. Edited by Xyooj Xeev Nruag. Wheaton, IL: Mong Voluntary Literacy Group.

--------. No date. *Lug Nruag Moob: Lug Nruag Lom Zem*/Humorous Folktales. Edited by Xyooj Xeev Nruag. Wheaton, IL: Mong Voluntary Literacy Group.

--------. No date. *Lug Nruag Moob: Lug Nruag Txa*/"Transformation" Folktales. Edited by Xyooj Xeev Nruag. Wheaton, IL: Mong Voluntary Literacy Group.

Thoj, Phaj, Khu Ntxawg Hawj, Nom Tooj Vaaj, and Xeev Nruag Xyooj. No date. *Lug Nruag Moob: Lug Nruag Tsuv*/"Tiger" Folktales. Edited by Xyooj Xeev Nruag. Wheaton, IL: Mong Voluntary Literacy Group.

Thoj Theeb, et al. 1981. *Phau Ntawv Dab Neeg Hmoob*/Book of Hmong Folktales. Sob Tuang, Thailand: The Ockenden Venture.

Thoj Maiv Yaj, and Txhiaj Tub. 1982. *Lub Ntiaj Teb*/The Earth, a geography text. Minneapolis, MN: Minneapolis Public Schools.

Tsav Nyiam Kawm Ntawv/Ja Likes to Study. No date. Ntawv Hmoob. Follows *Kawm Ntawv Hmoob* Books 1 and 2.

Tshoob Zawj. No date. *Piav Tus Txheej Txheem Kab Tshoob Kev Kos*/Marriage Procedures. Jackson, MO: Pragmatics International, Inc.

Vajtswv tej lus uas cawm neeg txojsia/Bible. 1981. Bangkok: The Bible Society of Thailand.

Vang, Gaohli Lyfoung. 1983. *Phau Nkauj Yexus Khetos*/Hmong Hymnal. Rockford, Illinois: Hmong Valley Baptist Church.

Vang, Lue, and Judy Lewis. 1984. *Grandmother's Path, Grandfather's Way*. Rancho Cordova, CA: Zellerbach Family Fund.

Vue, Pang Cher and Marilyn Anderson. 1982. *Hmoob Deskhauslas*/Hmong Decorah: Stories and Poems in Beginning English and Hmong. Decorah, IA: Northwest Iowa Technical Institute.

Vwj Tsawb, et. al, 1983. *Phau Qhia Nyeem Ntawv Hmoob Dawb*/Book to Teach White Hmong Reading. Washington, D.C.: Center for Applied Linguistics.

Xyooj Tsheej. 1981. *Phau Qhia Nyeem Tsiaj Ntawv Hmoob*/Book to Teach Reading the Hmong Alphabet. Denver, CO.

Xyooj Xeev Nruag, editor. 1981. *Kawm Ntawv Moob*/Learn (Green) Hmong. Wheaton, IL: Mong Voluntary Literacy Group.

----------. 1984. *Kawm Ntawv Moob, Phoo 2*/Learn(Green) Hmong, Book 2. Wheaton, IL: Mong Voluntary Literacy International, Inc.

----------. 1984. *Phoo/Phau Kawm Koom, Moob Leeg/Hmoob Dawb*/Book to Study Green Hmong and White Hmong Together. Wheaton, IL: Mong Voluntary Literacy Group.

Yaj Neeb. 1982. *Hmoob Cov Hnub Hauv Lipiam*/Hmong Days of the Week. Minneapolis, MN: Minneapolis Public Schools.

Yaj Neeb, and Lau Yang. 1982. *Kev Qhia Hauj Lwm*/Vocational Orientation. Minneapolis, MN: Minneapolis Public Schools.

Yaj, Neeb, Xeeb Lauj, and Laus Lis Txiab Lauj. 1982. *Kwv Huam Teb Chaws Asmesliskas*/U.S. History. Minneapolis: Minneapolis Public Schools,

Limited English Proficiency Program, Title VII Secondary. .

Yang, Dao. 1980. *Dictionnaire Française-Hmong Blanc*/French-White Hmong Dictionary. Paris: Comité National d'Entraide and Jacques Lemoine.

Zeb Xyooj Txooj Kaub. 1982. *Phau Xyaum Nyeem Zaj Lus*/Beginning Hmong Reader. Washington, D.C.: Center for Applied Linguistics.

Districts Ranked by Enrollment
of Limited-English Proficient Students
Who Speak Hmong

California law requires that school districts each year conduct a language census. The purpose of the census is to identify students who are considered to be limited-English proficient (LEP). Once identified, state law requires that LEP students be offered bilingual learning opportunities.

In the spring 1987, 13,103 students were reported to speak Hmong at home. Of these students, 10,780 or 82% percent were found to be of limited English proficiency and were classified as LEP. In addition to the 37 districts listed below that enroll 20 or more LEP Hmong speaking students, another 66 districts reported between 1 and 19 LEP students who speak Hmong.

DISTRICTS RANKED BY ENROLLMENT OF LEP STUDENTS
WHO SPEAK HMONG, SPRING, 1987

Name of School District	Rank by # of LEP (Hmong) students	LEP (Hmong) enrollmt Spring 1987	LEP (Hmong) students as a percentage of state LEP (Hmong) stds
Fresno Unified SD	1	3,479	32.3%
Merced City Elem SD	2	1,056	9.8
Stockton City Unified SD	3	1,005	9.3
Sacramento City Unified SD	4	818	7.6
San Diego Unified SD	5	517	4.8
Marysville Joint Union SD	6	424	3.9
Lodi Unified SD	7	286	2.7
Visalia Unified SD	8	257	2.4
Clovis Unified SD	9	254	2.4
Merced Union High SD	10	207	1.9
Banning Unified SD	11	201	1.9
Santa Ana Unified SD	12	181	1.7
Modesto City Elem SD	13	152	1.4

Long Beach Unified SD	14	140	1.3
North Sacramento SD	15	131	1.2
Grant Joint Union High SD	16	130	1.2
Eureka City Elem SD	17	99	0.9
Porterville Elem SD	18	96	0.9
Lompoc Unified SD	19	94	0.9
Weaver Union Elem SD	20	90	0.8
Atwater Elem SD	21	75	0.7
Folsom Cordova Unified SD	22	60	0.6
Garden Grove Unified SD	23	58	0.5
Thermalito Union Elem SD	24	54	0.5
Fairfield Suisun Unified SD	25	54	0.5
Lincoln Unified SD	26	49	0.5
Chico Unified SD	27	46	0.4
Del Paso Heights Elem SD	28	46	0.4
Tulare City Elem SD	29	43	0.4
Yuba City Unified SD	30	42	0.4
Del Norte Co. Unified SD	31	41	0.4
Rio Linda Union Elem SD	32	41	0.4
Goleta Union Elem SD	33	41	0.4
Oroville City Elem SD	34	35	0.3
Moreno Valley Unified SD	35	30	0.3
Santa Barbara City High SD	36	23	0.2
Ocean View Elem SD	37	20	0.2

Source: *DATA BICAL Report No. 87-7N*. Sacramento: California State Department of Education, Bilingual Education Office, Spring, 1987.

Educational Resources

❖Resource Centers

**Southeast Asian Refugee
Studies Project (SARS)**
Center for Urban and
Regional Affairs (CURA)
330 Hubert H. Humphrey Ctr
University of Minnesota
301 19th Avenue S.E.
Minneapolis, MN 55455

University Film and Video
University of Minnesota
1313 Fifth Street, S.E., Suite 108
Minneapolis, MN 55455
1-800-847-8251

**Center for South and Southeast
Asian Studies**
104 Lane Hall
University of Michigan
Ann Arbor, MI 48106

**Center for South and Southeast
Asian Studies**
260 Stephens Hall
University of California
Berkeley, CA 94720

Southeast Asia Program
Cornell University
120 Uris Hall
Ithaca, NY 14853

**Council on Southeast Asia
Studies**
Yale Center for International &
Area Studies,
Box 13A Yale Station
New Haven, CT 06520

The Cellar Bookshop
18090 Wyoming
Detroit, MI 48221

Asia Books
5 Sukhumvit Road Soi 61
Bangkok 10110, Thailand

❖Sources of Hmong Language Materials

Association Communauté Hmong
97318 Javouhey
FRANCE (Guyane fr.)

Center for Applied Linguistics
1118 22nd Street N.W.
Washington, D.C. 20037
202-429-9292

Department of Linguistics
Macalester College
1600 Grand Avenue
St. Paul, MN 55105

Mong Volunteer Literacy Group
P.O. Box 56
Winfield, IL 60190
(changed from Wheaton, IL)

Southeast Asia Community
Resource Center
Folsom Cordova Unified School
District
2562 Chassella Way, Room 10
Rancho Cordova, CA 95670
(916) 635-6815

Hmong Catholic Association
951 E. 5th Street
St. Paul, MN 55106

Southeast Asian Refugee
Studies Project (SARS)
Center for Urban and Regional
Affairs (CURA)
University of Minnesota
301 19th Avenue S.E.
Minneapolis, MN 55455

❖Human Resources:
Persons with Special Knowledge
of Hmong Language and Culture

Yves Bertrais
Association Communauté Hmong
97318 Javouhey
FRANCE (Guyane fr.)

Amy Catlin, Ph.D.
Ethnomusicology Department
University of California, Los Angeles
Los Angeles, CA 90024
213-825-7443

Gary Yia Lee, Ph.D.
School of Behavioural Sciences
MacQuarie University
New South Wales 2109
Australia

Bruce Bliatout, Ph.D.
Refugee Health Specialist
Health Services Division
426 S.W. Stark Street, 7th Floor
Portland, OR 97204   (503) 248-3674

Professor Timothy Dunnigan
Department of Anthropology
215 Ford Hall
University of Minnesota
224 Church Street S.E.
Minneapolis, MN 55455

Professor Jacques Lemoine
School of Advanced Studies in the
Social Sciences,
Paris, France

Charles Li
Department of Linguistics
University of California, Santa Barbara
Santa Barbara, CA

Dao Yang, Ph.D.
Help Center
50 Nicholson Hall
University of Minnesota
216 Pillsbury Drive
Minneapolis, MN 55455

Thomas Amis Lyman
3351 St. Helena Highway North
St. Helena, CA 94574

Professor Kenji Ima
Department of Sociology
San Diego State University
San Diego, CA 92182

❖ ❖

Hmong Community Organizations and Publications

❖California Hmong Organizations

Central Hmong American Association
8655 Hillery Drive
San Diego, CA 92126

Central Hmong American, Inc.
146 Olive Terrace
P.O. Box 552
Porterville, CA 93258

Hmong American Women's
Association, Inc.
358 Valeria, #20
Fresno, CA 93701

Hmong Association of Long Beach
1401 Chestnut Avenue, Room 323
Long Beach, CA 90813

Hmong Culture, Arts, Crafts
Teaching Museum
1136 Rivera Drive
Sacramento, CA 95838

Hmong Culture Collection, Inc.
2021 W. Dakota, #150-L
Fresno, CA 93705

Hmong Handicrafts
c/o Alliance for the Arts
842 North Fulton Avenue
Fresno, CA 93728

Hmong Student Association
of Fresno County, Inc.
1830 S. Chance, #B
Fresno, CA 93702

Hmong Student Association
of Sacramento, Inc
P.O. Box 423
Rancho Cordova, CA 95670

Hmong Student's Association
of Fresno State University
4969 N. Baker, #108
Fresno, CA 93726

Hmong Student Club
of Fresno City College
1101 E. University
Fresno, CA 93703

Lao Ethnic Association, Inc.
3233 Mayfair Boulevard
Fresno, CA 93702

Lao Family Community, Inc.
501 Westward Avenue
Banning, CA 92220

Lao Family Community, Inc.
3121 E. Olive Street
Fresno, CA 93702

Lao Family Community, Inc.
855 West 15th Street
Merced, CA 95340

Lao Family Community, Inc.
905 Valente Way
Modesto, CA 95351

Lao Family Community, Inc.
2270 Alessandro Blvd, Ste B
Moreno Valley, CA 92388

Lao Family Community, Inc.
P.O. Box 11162
San Diego, CA 92111

Lao Family Community, Inc.
529 North Sutter Avenue
Stockton, CA 95202

Lao Freedom Association, Inc.
4527 E. Belmont
Fresno, CA 93702

Southeast Asian Farm
Development Center
P.O. Box 10154
Stockton, CA 95210

The Xiong Educational Way
4624 E. Lane
Fresno, CA 93702

Lao Family Community, Inc.
5840 Franklin Blvd
Sacramento, CA 95824

Lao Family Community, Inc.
1140 South Bristol Street
Santa Ana, CA 92704

Lao Family Community of Tulare
247 W. Ferguson
Visalia, CA 93291

Lao Hmong Security Agency
11582 Trask Avenue
Garden Grove, CA 92643

United Xiong Ancestry
Assistance Association, Inc.
P.O. Box 3791
Merced, CA 95344

Yim Hmoob Educational
Association
P.O. Box 5239
San Diego, CA 92105

❖Publications

Haiv Hmoob (Magazine)
Dao Yang, editor
P.O. Box 11314
Minneapolis, MN 55411

❖❖❖❖❖❖❖❖❖❖❖❖❖❖❖❖❖

Hmong Linguistic Tables

Table D.1 RPA Spelling and Pronunciation of White Hmong Consonants

		Bilabial	Bilabial (w/lateral release)	Labio-dental	Apico-dental	Apico-dental (Affricated)	Lamino-dental- Palatal Offglide	Apico-alveolar	Lamino-alveolar	Apico-post-alveolar w/ rhotic release	Palatal	Velar	Uvular	Glottal
Stops and Affricates	Voiceless Unaspirated	p [p]	pl [pˡ]		t [t̪]	tx [t̪s̪]	c [t̠]	d [d̪ˑ]	ts [t̠ʃ]	r [ʈ]		k [k]	q [q]	[ʔ]
	Voiceless Aspirated	ph [pʰ]	plh [pˡʰ]		th [t̪ʰ]	txh [t̪s̪ʰ]	ch [t̠ʰ]	dh [d̪ʰˑ]	tsh [t̠ʃʰ]	rh [ʈʰ]		kh [kʰ]	qh [qʰ]	
	Pre-nasalized	np [mb]	npl [mbˡ]		nt [nd̪]	ntx [nd̪z̪]	nc [nd̠]		nts [nd̠ʒ]	nr [ɳɖ]		nk [ŋg]	nq [ɴɢ]	
	Pre-nasalized w/Aspiration	nph [mpʰ]	nplh [mpˡ̥]		nth [nt̪ʰ]	ntxh [nt̪s̪ʰ]	nch [nt̠ʰ]		ntsh [nt̠ʃʰ]	nrh [ɳʈʰ]		nkh [ŋkʰ]	nqh [ɴqʰ]	
Fricatives	Voiced			v [v]					z [ʒ]		xy [ʑ]	g [ɣ]		
	Voiceless			f [f]	x [ʂ]				s [ʃ]					h [h]
Nasals	Voiced	m [m]	ml [mˡ]		n [n̪]						ny [ɲ]			
	Voiceless	hm [m̥]	hml [m̥ˡ]		hn [n̥]						hny [ɲ̥]			
Liquids	Voiced				l [l]									
	Voiceless				hl [l̥]									
Glides											y [j]			

(From Ratliff 1986, p. 16, based on Jarkey.)

Table D.2 Spelling and Pronunciation of White Hmong Vowels

	MONOPHTHONGS		DIPHTHONGS
	FRONT	BACK	OPENING
	i [i]	w [ɨ] u [u̹]	i ⟶ a [iə] [ɨə] [uə]
	e [e]	o [ɔ̹]	
	ee [ɛ̃ŋ]	oo [ɔ̃ŋ]	CLOSING
		a [ə]	i ⟶ u [ai] [iə] / aɯ [aɯ] / au [aɯ]

(From Ratliff 1986, p. 18, based on Jarkey 1986.)

119

Table D.3 The Sounds of English

(sounds shown in boxes have no close equivalent in Hmong)

ENGLISH CONSONANTS

STOPS & AFFRICATES

b	d	ǰ	g		bill	dill	Jill	gill
pʰ	tʰ	čʰ	kʰ		pin	tin	chin	kin

FRICATIVES

v	ð	z	ž			vat	that	zap	leisure
f	θ	s	š	h		fin	thin	sin	shin	him

NASALS

m	n	ŋ		map	nap	sinking

LIQUIDS

l	r		load road

GLIDES

y	w		yard win

ENGLISH VOWELS

	FRONT	CENTRAL	BACK				
HIGH	iy		uw		seen		soon
	I	ɨ	U		pit	roses	put
	ey		ow		bay		bow
MID	ɛ	ə	ɔ		bet	cut	bought
LOW	æ	a			bat	pot	

DIPHTHONGS	aw	ay	oy		pout	pipe	boy

STRESS e.g.,

export	vs.	export
reference	vs.	refer
proclamation	vs.	proclaim

Appendix E

Holidays and Special Events Celebrated in the Hmong Community

It is difficult to determine the Hmong holidays. They vary from one area to another, from one country to another. Generally, there are three categories of holidays among the Hmong people of Laos.

❖NATIONAL HMONG HOLIDAY (*XYOO TSHIAB*)

Only the Hmong New Year (*xyoo tshiab*) is considered as the national Hmong holiday. It is preceded by a series of ritual ceremonies on the 30th day of the 12th month of the Hmong lunar calendar (*tsiab peb caug*). It falls approximately between the 25th of November and the 25th of December each year. The celebration of the Hmong New Year lasts from three to seven days. However, some Hmong delay the New Year celebration because of harvest priorities. In the U.S. the Hmong refugees often celebrate the Hmong New Year at different times because of the weather or the difficulties of finding a place in which to gather the Hmong communities.

❖REGIONAL HMONG HOLIDAYS

Tsa Hauv Toj Ceremony

To attract divine blessings, some Hmong villages organize the *tsa hauv toj* ceremony. It consists of erecting a long bamboo pole, the top of which is tied with a red fabric ribbon. One or several buffaloes or cows are killed in sacrifice to the local spirits to ensure their blessings for prosperity, good health, and safety. The *tsa hauv toj* ceremony lasts one day and is attended by all the villages in the area.

Noj Txhooj Ceremony

To better administrate their populations, some Hmong local leaders call their subordinates and their subjects to a *noj txhooj*. It is a political meeting in which regulations regarding taxes, community services, agricultural activities, marriage rules, etc., are discussed, amended or renewed for another three year term. At this occasion, the local leaders kill one or several buffaloes or cows to entertain the guests. This event lasts one day.

❖INDIVIDUAL HMONG HOLIDAYS

Hnub Caiv Sab Mob Sab Ntsaj

When a Hmong person has a nightmare, he goes to see a shaman. The latter, after consulting his spirits, asks the man to observe one or more specific days which are called "ill-fated" days or *hnub caiv sab caiv ntsaj*. If he fails to observe those days, he might become ill, have a serious accident, or die. During those periods of time, he and all members of his family cannot do any work outside the family home. They cannot go out of the house and cannot receive any visitors. They erect two small branches partially stripped of leaves, one at each entrance of the house, to notify visitors.

Xyom Niam Xyom Txiv Hnub Tuag

Some Hmong observe a memorial ceremony, or *xyom niam xyom txiv hnub tuag* as a sign of respect to their parents on each anniversary of their deaths. On these days they kill a chicken in sacrifice, burn paper money for their parents' souls, and stop all agricultural activities.

Hu Plig Ceremony

Traditionally, three days after the birth of a child, the parents organize a *hu plig* or "calling the soul" ceremony for the baby. A shaman calls the soul of the new-born to join his or her family, and gives the baby a name. Then he expresses gratitude to the couple, *poj dab pog*, the spirits who brought the new-born to his parents, and invites the ancestors to participate in the feast offered at this occasion. The *hu plig* ends with wishes and blessings, symbolized by cotton strings tied around the wrists of the baby and the parents by relatives and friends.

Noj Tshoob Ceremony

When a young man and a young woman decide to marry, their families organize a *noj tshoob* or wedding ceremony. It is always preceded by long negotiations which last two or three days, and ends with a wedding feast gathering together members of the bride's and the groom's families, relatives and friends.

Tis Npe Laus Ceremony

Generally after the birth of the third child, the young father kills a pig and invites his parents-in-law to a *tis npe laus* ceremony. The purpose is for the parents-in-law to choose an "adult" name which is added to the father's other name. This signifies that the young man has entered the adult world, and is worthy of respect. Relatives and friends are invited to the ceremony which ends with wishes for good health, longevity, and prosperity for the young father and his family.

Pam Tuag Ceremony

The *pam tuag* or burial ceremony is the most important event in the Hmong society. The reason for having sons is to ensure a proper and worthy burial for the parents. It may last several days, sometimes several weeks, to allow members of the deceased person's family, relatives and friends from all parts of the country and from all over the world to come pay their last respects to the man or woman who has begun the long trip to the "country of the ancestors". Several pigs and bulls are killed in sacrifice to the dead person and served to the hundreds or thousands of participants. Only after the body is carried to the grave do the people scatter and return home.

Appendix F

❖ ❖ ❖ ❖ ❖ ❖

Glossary

additive bilingualism— A process by which individuals develop proficiency in a second language subsequent to or simultaneously with the development of proficiency in the primary language.

affective filter— The screening effects of personality, motivation, and other feelings on the reception or expression of a second language. The filter is high when when the learner is tense, uncomfortable, or defensive, but low when the learner is comfortable and receptive. A high filter diminishes the amount of comprehensible input.

American Cultural Orientation course (CO)— A course offered in Phanat Nikhom refugee camp in Thailand (and elsewhere) for refugees accepted for resettlement in the United States, designed to develop basic survival skills. Classes are taught by indigenous staff, supervised by American teachers.

basic interpersonal communicative skills— Second language skills that are equivalent to the ordinary conversational fluency of native speakers. These skills are normally acquired in the home or community, and are necessary but not sufficient grounds for academic success.

bilingual education program— An organized curriculum the includes (Hmong) language development, English language learning, and school subject learning through both Hmong and English. Adds the goal of bilingualism/biliteracy to the other school goals.

Black Hmong— Name used by others for some White Hmong.

Blue Hmong— Same as Green Hmong.

clan— A group of families of whom claim descent from the same mythological ancestor. There are approximately twenty different Hmong clans, with names like Lee, Vang, Xiong, and Yang.

classifier— see *noun classifiers*.

cognitive/academic language proficiency— Language skills associated with literacy and academic achievement. Includes greater vocabulary, more complicated syntax, and a higher level of abstraction than does "basic interpersonal communicative skills".

communicative-based English as a Second Language— One approach to teaching English as a second language; student progress is measured by ability to communicate messages in English; the focus is on language function and not on formal grammar; the "natural approach" is one such approach.

comprehensible input— Language that enters the learner's brain (listening or reading) which is largely comprehensible; the teacher provides an environment, materials, and strategies that increase the comprehensibility of the language. Examples include using realia, photographs, gestures, etc. Krashen holds that language acquisition takes place when there's comprehensible input.

grammar-based English as a Second Language— One approach to teaching English as a Second Language which is based on teaching the grammar of the language; student progress is measured by how well they form grammatically correct language output (speaking or writing). Examples of this approach are the grammar-translation method, the audiolingual method, and the cognitive code.

Green Hmong (*Moob Ntsuab*)— A subgroup of the Hmong people; the dialect they speak.

highland tribes— Any of several distinct ethnic groups living principally in the higher elevations in Laos, and including the Hmong, Mien, Black Thai, and several other tribal groups.

highland Lao— A member or members of any of several highland tribes of Laos, including the Hmong, Iu Mien and others.

Hmong Daw (*Hmoob Dawb*)— White Hmong; the English spelling of the Hmong name.

Hmongic languages— A group of related languages of China and Southeast Asia including the Hmong language.

Hmoob— White Hmong spelling of the word Hmong.

immersion program— An organized curriculum in which the students study in a second language, including literacy in the second language and subject area study via the second language; native language development is also part of the program; in addition to the regular school goals, an additional goal is that of proficient bilingualism. English speakers living in French Canada often participate in immersion French programs.

Iu Mien— An alternate name for the Mien. A highland people of Laos; their language, closely related to the Hmong language.

Khmu— An indigenous people of Laos, living at middle elevations.

Lao— The majority population of Laos; their language, closely related to Thai, the national language of Thailand.

Laos— A land-locked nation of mainland Southeast Asia, bordered by China, Vietnam, Cambodia, Thailand, and Burma; the homeland of the Hmong in the United States.

Laotian— Pertaining to the nation of Laos, e.g., the Laotian government, a Laotian citizen.

liquid— A class of consonant sounds, including [l] and [r].

limited bilingualism— A form of subtractive bilingualism; the learner is not an educated native speaker of either the native or the second language; basic interpersonal communicative skills in the two languages, but the cognitive/academic skills in neither.

lowland Lao— Lao, the ethnic identification and language of the majority group of Laos.

Meo— Name for the Hmong people used by others in Southeast Asia, considered derogatory by the Hmong.

Miao— Chinese name for the Hmong people, considered derogatory by the Hmong in America.

Mien— A highland people of Laos also called *Iu Mien*; their language, closely related to the Hmong language.

Mong— English spelling of the word Hmong, reflecting Green Hmong pronunciation; Green Hmong.

Mong Leng (*Moob Leeg*)— Same as Mong Njua, or Green Hmong.

Mong Njua (*Moob Ntsuab*)— Green Hmong; English spelling of the name as pronounced in Green Hmong.

monitor— The "watchdog" of spoken or written language; the process by which a person processes, stores, and retrieves conscious rules of languages.

monosyllabic— In a monosyllabic language, words always or nearly always consist of only one syllable, e.g., Hmong, *qeej, pa, ndao.*

Moob— Green Hmong dialect spelling of the word Hmong (Mong).

morpheme— The smallest part of a word that has a meaning. The word *potato* has one morpheme; the word *misspelled* has three morphemes: *mis- + spell + -ed.*

morphology— Principles of word-formation.

mutual assistance association (MAA)— This is the term most commonly used to describe membership and service organizations in the United States operated by and providing services for refugees.

nasal— A stop consonant that is pre-nasalized (q.v.) or characterized by airflow through the nose; [m] and [n] are nasal consonants.

noun classifiers— A set of words, in some languages, that are used with nouns and that typically express a semantic class to which the noun belongs, e.g., human, round, long, flat.

numeral classifiers— Same as *noun classifiers*

pa ndao (*paj ntaub*)— Literally, *flower cloth*; the intricate needlework and batik produced by Hmong artisans, usually women.

partial bilingualism— Level of proficiency in two languages in which the learner has native-like proficiency (able to comprehend, speak, read and write) in one language but not the other.

pre-nasalization— A nasal onset (initial *m-, n-,* or *ng*-like sound) found in certain stop consonants in Hmong or other languages, spelled with initial *n* in Hmong.

proficient bilingualism— Level of bilingualism in which the learner has native-like proficiency (ability to comprehend, speak, read, and write) in two languages.

qeej— A Hmong wind instrument used for entertainment and for funeral and other ceremonies.

roman alphabet— The alphabet originally developed for Latin, used in modern forms to write English and other European languages, as well as Turkish, Chinese (pinyin), Vietnamese, Hmong, and other languages.

Romanized Practical Alphabet (RPA)— A roman alphabet developed as a practical orthography for the Hmong language by American and French missionaries in Laos and Thailand in the 1950's. The RPA is the writing system most commonly used by Hmong in the United States, France, and Australia. The alphabet is used for both White Hmong and Green Hmong dialects, sometimes with variant spellings.

secret war of Laos— The military conflict between forces of the Royal Lao government, supported by the United States government through the CIA, and Communist Pathet Lao and Vietnamese forces backed by North Vietnam, lasting approximately from 1962 to 1973.

serial verb construction— The use of two or more verbs, with no conjunction between them, in a single clause. English example: "Let's *go eat*."

sheltered English classes— One approach to teaching subject matter through a second language (English), in which the language input is made more comprehensible; this approach uses techniques like grouping students with similar English proficiencies, altering the complex reading material to fit the students' level, and teaching the aspects that pertain to second language learners, but not native speakers.

submersion classes— Second language learners in regular subject matter classes; the language is "native to native", with few alterations in materials or methods to make the language input more comprehensible.

submersion program— An organized curriculum that is designed for native English speakers (the "regular school program"), but that is often used with second language learners.

subtractive bilingualism— A form of bilingualism in which the acquisition of one language (usually the native language) is interrupted or suppressed; the learner has poor proficiency of the native language, or a complete loss of the native language.

tone, lexical— Distinctive voice pitch associated with a word or morpheme, by which one word may be distinguished from another. Hmong has seven distinct lexical tones.

transitional bilingual education program— An organized curriculum in which the native language (Hmong) is used in a systematic way for some period of time after the learner enters school.

voiced— pronounced with vocal cord vibration ("voicing"), like English *v, d, m, l*, etc. All vowels are voiced.

voiceless— pronounced without vocal cord vibration, like English *f, t*, etc. People who pronounce *Y* (or *wye*) and *why* the same have voiced *w* (*wh*) in both; people who pronounce them differently have a voiceless *w* (*wh*) in *why*. Also called "unvoiced".

White Hmong (*Hmoob Dawb*)— A subgroup of the Hmong people; the dialect they speak.

Yao— Name used by outsiders to refer to the Mien (q.v.).